Soul Moments

Times When Heaven Touches Earth

Soul Moments

Times When Heaven Touches Earth

Isabel Anders

ThomasMore®
– An RCL Company –
Allen, Texas

Contents

Acknowledgment:
Scriptural quotes taken from the *New Revised Standard Version.* Some of
the material in chapters 2, 11, and 17 has appeared in another form in
*Synthesis: A Weekly Resource for Preaching and Worship in the Episcopal
Tradition* (Dec. 27, 1998; Jan. 31, 1999; and Feb. 14, 1999).
Used by permission of Sedgwick Publishing Co., P. O. Box 328, Boyds,
MD 20841.

Send all inquiries to:
Thomas More
An RCL Company
200 East Bethany Drive
Allen, Texas 75002-3804

BOOKSTORES:
    Call Bookworld Companies 888-444-2524 or fax 941-753-9396
PARISHES AND SCHOOLS:
    Thomas More Publishing 800-822-6701 or fax 800-688-8356
INTERNATIONAL:
    Fax Thomas More Publishing 972-264-3719

Visit our website at **www.rclweb.com**

Printed in the United States of America

Library of Congress Catalog Card Number: 99-74606

ISBN 0-88347-430-1

1 2 3 4 5   03 02 01 00 99

To Bill

for all the moments . . .

Introduction:
The Slippery Soul

I have calmed and quieted my soul,
like a weaned child with its mother;
my soul is like the weaned child
that is with me.

—Psalm 131:2

Teach me wisdom in my secret heart.
—Psalm 51:6

What is the soul? It's who I am—
again—when I awake from the tangled
web of confusing dreams that have
swept me through a soulful night and on
toward dawn. Still half-immersed in that shadow life
that I assume each night "undercover," I emerge
grasping a fleeting handful of images and scenes—but it
is a losing battle. My body takes shape once again as
who I am in wakeful life, eyes start to focus on the
available light, morning tasks appear like lists to be
tackled . . . and I am my conscious self.

But how and why do I truly believe that something
soulful has occurred quite beyond my control or—
now—even my full remembrance? Have I really had the
experience of being taught truth in my inward being,
wisdom in my "secret heart"?

Once, in what had begun as a fitful night, I was
granted a dream. I was driving a car, alone, through some
long, circuitous countryside route, but with an inner
knowledge that I would safely arrive at my destination.
The effort and the time spent on the road were part and
parcel of the appreciation I would feel upon my arrival.

Once there, I entered into the most beautiful,
idyllic park or retreat grounds. I can still taste the sweet

assurance that the Management was not only waiting for me—I found that I truly belonged there and was expected. "It's all true . . . this is a foretaste . . . " was the thought of my heart, if not my actual verbal response. I had a consciousness, even while dreaming, of being given just the refreshment of spirit that I needed to go back to the frustrations of my work and decision-making and struggle to be good for the people around me. Just wishful thinking? Fantasizing? In a dream, we have no such control.

I see it instead as pure Gift. The aura of peace and fulfillment that I experienced—not just dreamed—has stayed with me through all these years. When I am tempted to doubt God's goodness, my experience confirms the life verse bestowed on me (along with all of my college graduating class): "I know the plans that I am planning for you . . . plans of welfare, and not of calamity, to give you a future and a hope" (Jeremiah 29:11, paraphrased).

The soul sometimes leads the way for the rest of me to follow.

Dreams and poetry and song could be called the language of the soul. "Rock-a my soul in the bosom of Abraham . . . " go lines of one spiritual. I couldn't explain the meaning of that line to save my theological life. But something in me "rocks" to it. Who I am at my core desires intensely to be "rocked"—to have Someone who calms and quiets my soul as though it were an infant, infinitely valued and held in love.

Without the connection our soul gives us to the eternal, we would truly be cut off. Recently our family of four huddled together in an inner closet while a just-spotted tornado passed over our county. We had with us a dead, useless cordless phone (later we discovered that our phone box had been hit directly by lightning, burning out that phone and its answering machine, but, mercifully, leaving the computers intact).

A dead phone is soul-less. Conversely, a computer with its hard disk intact—the Macintosh "happy face" appearing in sequence as it warms up, like a genie at-your-service, is a truly soul-assuring sight (when one depends on such technology to do daily work). We have some idea—and not only from technology—of what soul is when it is absent. Its departure is like the blankness behind an ailing face, the deadness of an uncircuited screen, the emptiness of a home from which love has fled. Who among us has not experienced this—at least temporarily?

But what is the soul, that slippery entity who is somehow "us" and that seems to have business beyond our conscious life? I cannot say, anymore than I know the color of the wind. But I see its effects all around: art, love, generativity—all human creativity, are signs that "soul was here."

Whatever woke me at 4 a.m. this morning to impel me to put words to paper had some soul in it—a desire to make a bridge from the richness of the deep in which I slept . . . to the daylight of accountability and communication.

I don't understand it. I only want to recognize soul moments when they occur, and to record some of them here . . . not as standards or expectations or spiritual laws . . . but simply as word-photographs captured when the soul least expected it.

Soul moments occur when two hearts touch, or a long-sought-after idea starts to gel in an exciting way, or events fall into the right sequence to allow for an action or decision, or—whenever we *feel* that there is more to this pause in time than appears on the surface of things. We stop . . . or look up . . . or soar. For the point of an infinitesimal moment, we have "come to ourself," and we simply *know:* the soul may be slippery and invisible and indefinable . . . but we are it.

For me, soul implies a vast web of interrelatedness, finding oneself not as autonomous, but as part of a vast pattern. Some mystics have likened that larger pictureto a great mansion, in which we are all component parts. Another, biblical image is a body, of which we are members, each with a function and purpose. Or we could be stars, fragments of the mother of all constellations.

I am not a mystic . . . but my roles as a wife, a mother, an editor, a writer, a citizen of the world have taught me that there is something to this ancient wisdom, something to tap into at all points of daily, sequential life. As a Christian, I seek to understand and define soul moments in the context of my belief, my faith in God and Christ.

Come with me through a series of soul moments— not necessarily in any kind of order—but each having some quality of opening up to that deeper, richer world that part of us knows like the palm of our own hand. We strengthen our soulfulness by continual immersion in ancient wisdom, in the arts, in the lives of our families and neighbors, and, I believe, in prayer: an ongoing dialog with the Creator, who nurtures and enlightens us as seeking human beings.

I don't have the answers. I am just a receptor— albeit (as we all are) a "fearfully and wonderfully made" receiver, a listener, a learner. It is my desire to discern and draw conclusions and find patterns that teach and lead me on to yet newer paths of learning and discovery, in those "vast fields of experience that await the soul"— Evelyn Underhill's fine expression.

Soul moments—times when heaven touches earth—are here and now, in the thick of things, sometimes occurring as we are most aware of our human limitations and confusion. They encircle us, and, for their moment, name us: loved, beloved, cherished, chosen. The experience passes, but the soul bears its indelible mark.

I am because God is. Somehow this very particularity with which I have been blessed has a place in the Divine purpose. Knowing this from my soul, I can go back to my work, my responsibilities, my life—refreshed, assured.

If these moments help you to identify your own soul moments in the past, and recognize them as they come to you in the days ahead, I will be gratified.

"Fuel Is Low"

The Lord turns a desert into pools of water, a parched land into springs of water . . .
rivers into a desert, springs of water into thirsty ground.

—Psalm 107:35, 33

Forest and field, sun and wind and sky,
earth and water, all speak the same quiet language.
—Thomas Merton

Chapter One

$\mathcal{W}$e live in rural Tennessee, far from the madding crowds. We enjoy the beauty of the mountains, the nearby lakes and recreation, and being able to park right in front of the post office even—usually—on a Monday morning. The local waitresses know your name, and even bank clerks tell you with Southern graciousness to "Come back!" (Where else would you go to retrieve your money?)

I have encountered only one rude salesperson in ten years. And it's safe to smile at passersby on the sidewalk . . .

As a transplanted midwesterner I also appreciate the rolling hills, the (usually) moderate weather, and the fact that you can see green somewhere in the landscape all year round. But there are drawbacks. In fact, people "back home" hardly believe me when I say that we go to another state to *seriously* shop. Of course there are malls in Tennessee, but the closest REAL one to us is on the other side of the Alabama border, in Huntsville, over an hour away.

One late winter evening several years ago, we were driving back through the farmlands and rural towns along the two-lane road that connects us to Alabama and our shopping haven. Driving a newly bought car that consumed only diesel fuel, we hadn't stopped to think about tanking up before we left the gas-station-studded outskirts of the city.

Now this was a car that amiably reminded us "Close left door!" and "Buckle up!" in an electronic generic woman's voice when we hadn't lived up to its standards. Something of a novelty. But when the she-voice of the car warned us about halfway home: "Fuel is low," it wasn't so easily satisfied.

By that time we were in the midst of a driving rain that barely allowed visibility of the few gas-station lights dotting the way home. And most of them, we now feared, didn't carry diesel. In the back seat, our younger daughter was fighting back tears, peering through the misty windows, determinedly trying to help us find an oasis.

Then, in the midst of her eight-year-old prayers (and ours), the rain suddenly stopped, and we pulled easily into the next station—one we hadn't remembered being there last time. As my husband pulled over to the diesel pump, off to one side of the building, I turned around to hug my girls and we whispered, "Thank you, Lord!"

It was a soul moment.

As much as I would insist that prayer isn't like a slot machine in which you insert your coins and hold out your palms for the bounty to pour in to them—*we had prayed and God had answered.* What more was there to say?

Instead of having to sit by the side of a darkened two-lane road waiting for help—we were filled, and on our way to the warmth and welcome of home and rest and familiarity after a satisfying day.

As adults, we took this incident in stride, having seen more than once how—in much more serious circumstances—God can turn a desert into pools of water, a parched land into springs . . . We try to live expectantly and thankfully—even when our immediate prospects are diminished for a time, and rivers temporarily waste into a desert . . . and it seems as though the Lord has turned, before us, springs of water into thirsty ground . . . But for our daughter, in her sensitive, impressionable soul, this particular answered prayer was a milestone. "God heard us, Mama!"

As a parent, no matter how much you want to teach a child about faith, and SHOW her how it works in real life . . . the props are simply too big and unwieldy, the circumstances too intractable. We are, as adults, just as stuck in the midst of the plot—with its unpredictable, jarring stops and shifts and fluctuations—as are our children.

No doubt that is because *we too,* at our core, *are* children, dependent always on our heavenly Father who "clothes the grass of the field" and tends the toil-less lilies. And feeds the diesel engines in their time . . .

Sometimes, it is out of just such soul moments that a life of faith begins to be built, stone by stone, to serve for us later as an altar of remembrance.

Our children are in bigger hands, held by sturdier, more "everlasting" arms than our own—thank God. All we can do sometimes, helpless as we find ourselves— and unable to take credit when we are rescued—is to stand at the spot and point.

God met us here. Thus far the Lord has helped us.

Of course, some of those "spots" are really *times:* days and seasons, of drought and harvest. We look back and remember in order to be able to claim the grace to move forward again.

We take a moment, in a dry and thirsty land, to remember that when "Fuel is low!" the Source that we need to fill-'er up again is somewhere out there, "fixing to" meet us on the road.

Seeds of Glory

All of us, with unveiled faces, seeing the glory of the Lord as though reflected in a mirror, are being transformed into the same image from one degree of glory to another . . .

—2 Corinthians 3:18

This mystery . . . is Christ in you, the hope of glory.
—Colossians 1:27

Chapter Two

$\mathcal{I}$t doesn't happen often . . . someone has described the look of a transfigured human face as "like alabaster with a light behind it."

But if we are indeed being transformed into God's image, from one degree of shining to another, then it is no wonder that shades of that glory may register—even to our eyes—from time to time here and now.

I have seen it rimming the beautiful elderly face of my friend Elizabeth, her feathery upswept hair gently framing that same face, like a cameo defying time. I feel from her the life that rings out from the glory, as I grasp small, thin fingers that still make the keys of her Steinway respond sweetly to their touch. The large corners and eaves of her formal drawing room overwhelm her small figure. But her presence draws one in to her . . . she is at the center of a kind of fire, a burning called obedience.

"I'm *not* going to give *up!*" she said to me recently, of her slow, determined—and amazing—recovery from last season's fall and broken hip. As though, *"How could anyone ever think that?"*

I have seen shades of glory in the unexplainable shine of her penetrating eyes when she is describing for me the contents of one of the fascinating books always stacked up in twos and threes on her coffee table. Various bookmarks jut out to measure how far she got before putting one down one and picking up another.

"This is marvelous," she points to a volume. She gleams like a child with unopened presents, unable to choose from the riches of these current historical works and fiction and devotional volumes . . . dipping in and out of their riches to "keep up." She is drawn irresistibly to books—and music, and art—that feed her ever-inquiring mind and ever-growing spirit.

"See, you can be like Miss Elizabeth," I have told my children. "You can always continue learning and discovering and growing, even in your nineties."

Glory in a drawing room . . . *Yes,* the experience says to us: *Here is the color of life.* I have been bathed in glory at points of common touch—when one of my children, glimpsing my face across a crowded room, has run with abandon into my outstretched arms.

It was just such a small scenario I observed once in my pre-children days: a little boy, aglow, zinging toward his mother like a magnet—that made my heart leap and desire to experience such a love someday. It was a soul moment for me, no less than—later, on one unbearably bleak day (of *real* abandonment)—when an unexpected fragment of a muted rainbow glimpsed *out of the blue* gave me faith that I *would* one day be the mother of children. . . . *Incandescence.* I have seen it on my husband's face as he spoke his vows to me once on a cloudless afternoon . . . and in his faithful, self-forgetting devotion to me on myriad occasions since.

In human faces and in earthly time, God makes known to us the riches of this mystery: Christ in us, the hope of glory. If the Kingdom is among us here and now, then it is no wonder that some of its characteristics will occasionally seep out—shine out—from the midst of our mundane, earthbound experience, reminding us of our true destiny.

The English poet and novelist Charles Williams has written of going to visit the renowned writer Evelyn Underhill after one of her bouts of illness. As he tells it, she was sitting facing a glowing fireplace. "As I entered she got up and turned round, looking . . . fragile. . . . *But* light simply streamed from her face illuminated with a radiant smile. . . . One could not help but feel consciously there and then (not on subsequent recognition or reflection) that one was in the presence of the extension of the Mystery of our Lord's Transfiguration in one of the members of His Mystical Body. I myself never saw it repeated on any later meeting . . . "[1]

Jesus himself set the pattern, gave us the prototype. He was seen as "transfigured" by three close disciples on a "high mountain" in the company of the no-doubt-also-glowing figures of Moses (whose skin had shone from being with God) and Elijah (who had cheated death by way of a fiery chariot taking the whirlwind route to heaven). Even his clothes were luminescent: dazzling white, such as no fuller on earth could bleach them. Seeds of glory come from another Place altogether.

Why should we be so amazed? Why should we stand gazing, gaping, staring? Surely the thin line that separates us from seeing what is there, under all our skin, is very thin and permeable. If the soul itself is by nature invisible, the glory of Presence is not.

But there is work to do. Not building altars on the spot. Usually, not kneeling either. A helping hand, a gentle smile, the consistency of compassion will do. It is immortals that we brush up against daily. We've just been given a reminder, is all.

But why us, why here, why now?

I think we are allowed to taste of the glory at times to remind us, in Evelyn Underhill's words, that "It is 'of faith' that God dwells in our souls 'by essence of grace.' Of course all spatial language is really unmeaning as applied to Him because He is pure Spirit and is present everywhere in His fullness. The mystics always say He indwells the 'ground of the soul' below the level of everyday consciousness, utterly distinct from and yet more present to us than we are to ourselves. Some find it easiest to withdraw and find Him in their souls and others to turn to Him as if He were the sun; both true, and neither adequate."[2]

The mystic Hildegard of Bingen spoke in her writings of the "principle of life, the divine seed, the mysterious essence." And Meister Eckhart, following on St. Peter's Epistle, celebrated this image of a seed that is meant to be developed within us. For both saints, the glory was not just for ourselves. It was the essence of compassion. In the words of Eckhart: "Whatever God does, the first outburst is always compassion." Glory as visible compassion!

We can never fully experience the glory here. Nor are we meant to. But, for such soul moments as we are granted, *Deo gratias*.

[1] From Williams' Introduction to *The Letters of Evelyn Underhill*, (London: Longmans, Green and Co., 1943).
[2] *The Letters of Evelyn Underhill*, p. 245.

Smokescreen

The Lord will deliver you from the snare of the fowler and from the deadly pestilence. . . . You will not fear the terror of the night, or the arrow that flies by day . . . or the destruction that wastes at noonday.

—Psalm 91:3–6

*The future will be different
if we make the present different.*
—Peter Maurin

Chapter Three

$\mathcal{A}$ll is gray, hazy. There is literally no visibility—*zip*—*none*. We are moving slow as a snail, creeping on wheels, mesmerized. I dare not STOP here, but to go forward is to drive blindly.

Yet I have no choice.

My older daughter, the "Trekkie," and I are driving into town to see the movie *Lost in Space* at our local theater. We didn't count on getting lost in smoke ourselves on the way there! But someone is tending—more like neglecting—a huge conflagration of dry leaves just off the shoulder of the winding rural road. This fire has generated an out-of-control smokescreen, which has expanded and now blocks both lanes of the highway.

There is no turning around, it is too late. No alternate routes exist. There is nowhere else to go but straight through the cloud, blind as bats. I grip the wheel and lean forward tensely, telling Sarah, *"Pray we don't hit anything! We've just got to plow through this!"*

It all seemed like at least ten times as long as the minute-and-a-half or so it probably took us to reach the edge of the smokescreen and enter the crisp, clear, welcoming daylight.

I untensed all in a sigh. Undaunted, thankful, and immersed again in the normal perils of Saturday traffic—we trekked on to face the big-screen saga of mad robots and maniacs, techno-thrills and sappy dialogue. Relief quickly faded into enjoyment as we entered into the greater dilemma of a dysfunctional space family!

But this I know: I don't like it when I can't see where I'm going!

If a perfect summer's day can turn into a tunnel of impenetrable haze in a split-second, surely nothing, not even walking out one's front door, is safe. In fact, in childhood, I used to have fantasies, no doubt nursed by some frontier story I had read, of Indians at our front door: fiercely coming at us from the open field across from our suburban ranch house.

Whether that was a dream I had or a daytime musing, I can't remember. I do know that moments of lostness, and blindness, and inability to move one's limbs despite an approaching terror, are known territory to the soul. The Psalmist assures us that the Lord will deliver us from all manner of threats—in any state of our soul's awareness.

What a relief it often is to wake from night-terrors . . . as it was also to emerge from a daytime smoke-screen. This is but a picture—though a real experience—of other moments of true battle against the dark I have known, and of the excruciating, seemingly unrelieved effort to *continue* to affirm God's goodness and love for me.

Contrasts: night and day, siege and deliverance, imprisonment and glorious freedom, are reminders that weeping may linger for the night, but joy comes with the morning. The story goes on and on . . . the one we've been cast in. And *anything* can pop out at us, just around the bend.

The bad news for the soul is that we're never totally "out of the woods" in this life. The good news is that *this is what life is:* the trekking on, the courage, the doubts, the stamina, the occasional blindness, the willingness to ask for help as we need it on the way.

God the Lord is our rock and our fortress; whom shall we fear? An appropriate petition to carry in our hearts on the journey has also been phrased by saints of the past as simply, *"Lord, have mercy!"* As a soul-prayer, it is a one-size-fits-all-occasions refrain. Don't leave home without it.

Soul moments aren't always the warm, comfortable touches we would like as reassurance that all is, for the moment, well and right. Sometimes they come to us as sudden stabs of realization that that spare entity we call "faith" needs to be retrieved from our back pocket for *just such an instance as this!* It's kind of a gulp, a stop-in-your-tracks-for-a-moment jolt.

I've always said I believe. Now, what I so blithely affirmed in the light has to be appropriated right here in the dark. Oops. I didn't expect it to be THIS dark . . . or soon . . . or scary.

A short trip through a dark patch with no visible means of support. Most of us have been there. We can hardly call it a "dark night of the soul." But it is at least a lesser cousin. Perhaps if we had more faith, a backpack-load rather than a pocketful, we would experience an even greater test of our mettle. Some travelers have; others will yet, further down the pike.

The principle is the same. Hold on for all you're worth and keep on keeping on! The soul is made of sturdy stuff, if all the stories are true. Many have survived to tell their tales in the land of the living. *It is you who lights my lamp; O Lord, my God, you light up my darkness.*

A Book-Life

Here I am; in the scroll of the book it is written of me. I delight to do your will, O my God; your law is within my heart.

—Psalm 40:7–8

God usually answers our prayers so much more according to the measure of his own magnificence than of our asking that we do not know his boons to be those for which we besought him.

—Coventry Patmore,
The Rod, the Root, and the Flower

Chapter Four

$\mathcal{B}$ooks and the soul have been connected for me for as long as I can remember—from early days of being told with reverence that the Bible was "God's Book" . . . to the time when I began to read the Psalms in high school (encouraged by my father, who has read at least one Psalm every day of his adult life). . . . Later I discovered some of the "mystics" who actually sought to record for us the unfathomable: their intimate encounters with the Holy, their souls' experience of their God.

Seeking to write about the soul is tenuous ground at best. It is certainly possible to seek to overexplain. Dionysius the Areopagite wrote in *Mystical Theology*, that as one "raises himself towards Heaven, so his view of the spiritual world becomes simplified and his words fewer." No wonder St. Thomas Aquinas (c. 1225–1274), for all the brilliance and logic of his *Summa Theologica*, considered all he had written as mere straw, compared to his soul's encounter with God.

There is danger in seeking to comprehensively record the soul's experience. There is also danger in being unfaithful to the gift that we are sometimes given—of being told, "Take, write . . . " for our own understanding and for sharing with others. It is meet and right to take note of some of the signposts along the way that have made us say, "Something happened . . . my soul was enlarged, God touched me in a new way. *My soul, like Mary's, magnifies the Lord . . . "*

Why write about soul moments, sometimes the most ordinary events with a "spin" on them—a sudden insight, a pulling back of a veil that usually denies us a look at the eternal?

As G. K. Chesterton wrote in his marvelous life of St. Thomas, *The Dumb Ox:* "St. Thomas takes the view that the souls of all the ordinary hard-working and simple-minded people are quite as important as the souls of thinkers and truth-seekers; and he asks how all these people are possibly to find time for the amount of reasoning that is needed to find truth. . . . The *conclusion* he draws from it is that [people] must receive the highest moral truths in a miraculous manner"—or most of us would never receive them at all.*

Our experiences of the transcendent matter. God is reaching us through our soul moments.

But can experience really *teach* us in an authoritative way? I confess my prejudice for book learning. We are all four self-confessed "bookaholics" in this household. My husband has been caught commenting wryly that if the "book police" knew about our hoarding of volumes we'd surely be victims of a raid.

I love to see God's promises in print. I read in Psalm 40 the metaphor (recurring in Isaiah and Ezekiel and Daniel and Revelation) that perhaps God even has a sort of book, a scroll recording something of our soul's relationship to the eternal. It is an exciting and sometimes a chilling thought! What are we "writing" with our life?

As an editor, I like to have the last look at what goes in print—and such a book would be infinitely out of my hands. But I believe we *do* have free will—to recognize God's work and cooperate with it. I can only begin where I am today, to "write" my life differently, to enfold into the pages of my soul's experience a deeper commitment, a more sincere longing for God, and greater dedication to the Kingdom.

I can listen more carefully to the voices of the souls around me—those seeking comfort or advice or just a friend to listen. I can stop putting off the down-and-dirty tasks that lurk in my mind as a kind of "Do I have to?" list.

I can ask for eyes to see and ears to hear what is truly going on around me—even when it sounds to the ear like dissonance, threatening my peace, challenging my conscience.

There is work to be done, and it is not for the half-hearted. Our souls are created to be robust and resilient. And so, like the Psalmist, I seek the sure confidence that *all the pathways of the Lord are love and faithfulness.* I know deep within that I should not fear to walk on.

I can't edit out what has gone before. I can only seek to travel more deliberately, more faithfully. I can show my sincerity of heart by the choices I make today: by seeking God's guidance as I begin my day's work; by letting my mouth speak blessings as easily as I normally complain of a myriad woes.

Ronald Knox wrote: "It is painfully true that small things do matter; and it is in small things that we are always missing the opportunities which grace offers us."

And so, with all souls who long for communion with God, I seek to measure my soul's moments by days, as did the Psalmist in Psalm 42:

"By day the Lord commands his steadfast love,
and at night his song is with me,
a prayer to the God of my life . . . "

Here I am; in the scroll of the book it is written of me. I delight to do your will, O my God.

---

*G. K. Chesterton, *Saint Thomas Aquinas: The Dumb Ox* (New York: Image Books, 1956), p. 38.

A Local Food-Chain

O give thanks to the Lord, for he is good . . .
who gives food to all flesh,
for his steadfast love endures forever.

—Psalm 136:1, 25

Give me neither poverty nor riches;
feed me with the food that I need,
or I shall be full, and deny you, and say,
"Who is the Lord?"
or I shall be poor, and steal, and profane the name
of my God.

—Proverbs 30: 8–9

Above all, give us grace to live as true folk——to fast till we come to a refreshed sense of what we have and then to dine gratefully on all that comes to hand.

—Robert Farrar Capon

Chapter Five

$\mathcal{E}$arly mornings around here are punctuated by two predictables: Kit the Cat moans lugubriously in her mock-Siamese voice (she is a "common" tabby) at the front door, demanding her Friskies. Simultaneously, Larabee, our part-border collie/part-Welsh corgi, waits patiently outside the sliding glass door to the backyard—leaning up against the house as close as he can get. When one of us (usually my husband) opens the door to pet him and praise him and reach for his dish to wash and fill it—he is *infinitely* grateful, never piqued or uninterested. He rolls over onto his back right in your path and receives any petting with doggy sighs of fulfillment.

In fact, both cat and dog clearly prefer love with their morning meal. Stroking and scratching their fur is always a close second to the supplying of the food itself.

It is simply a fact of life that no one can live by bread alone. Oh, we need the sustenance on a regular basis, and we have our preferences as to how it is prepared and served. It seems some days that much of caring for a family is careful meal-planning, timing, and the inevitable cleanup. But eating is not what we are here for. Food sustains us in this life so that, paradoxically, our soul can have the freedom to yearn for *its* necessary fare—and be filled.

There is a sort of hierarchy in what we might refer to as the "food-chain" of life. C. S. Lewis wrote in *Mere Christianity* about how everything that God has made has some likeness to God. "Space is like Him in its hugeness. . . . Matter is like God in having energy. . . . The vegetable world is like Him because it is alive, and He is the 'living God.' But life, in this biological sense, is not the same as the life there is in God: it is only a kind of symbol or shadow of it.

"When we come to the animals, we find other kinds of resemblance in addition to biological life. The intense activity and fertility of the insects, for example, is a first dim resemblance to the unceasing activity and the creativeness of God. In the higher mammals we get the beginnings of instinctive affection. . . . When we come to man . . . we get the completest resemblance to God which we know of. . . . Man not only lives, but loves and reasons . . ."*

Lewis goes on to show that we use the word "life" in two ways when it refers to humans. One is the gift of natural life, the biological gifts which we share with the animals and other life—but which is more highly developed in us. The other "Life" is spiritual life—that which has had its source in God from all eternity. The first he calls *Bios*, the second, *Zoe*. He points out that a person who has "changed from having *Bios* to having *Zoe*"—in other words, who has come alive in the spirit— "would have gone through as big a change as a statue which changed from being a carved stone" to being a real human being.

These too are "mere" metaphors. No alive human being is really a statue. Our biological life drives us in many ways, and it seems as though some people seldom ask why they have been given that life in the first place. They hold out their bowl, so to speak, for the next meal. But their souls may be starving for lack of proper sustenance.

We have seen in our present culture the evidence of much hunger for soul-food, and people attempting to find it everywhere—from New Age literature and cultic experience, to self-styled nature worship, to a return to traditional mainline churches. It seems everyone is seeking more than bread.

In our yard, the food-chain is simple. When Kit doesn't get her crunchies put in the bowl on her preferred schedule, she will catch and maul a mouse, or a small chipmunk or bird, and leave its tattered remains on our doorstep. And who says animals can't speak? This little demonstration says, in bold letters: *YOU FAILED! But I coped anyway, clever cat that I am. So praise me.*

And we do. (When she leaves some of her prepared food, the slugs that crawl to it benefit in their own way. What feeds on them?)

Larabee, more restricted by his fenced environment, would no doubt be glad to make Kit an example of this "eat-the-next-size-down" principle—if he could get to her. But he manages instead on a canned-soy-chunks-with-gravy diet, and his allotment of human love . . . and peace is kept.

It seems fitting that the food-chain metaphor has recently been used of our national political (and economic) scene. It smacks of a life-view that sees *Bios* as an end in itself: MY concerns, MY fame, MY winning . . .

Yet what if our end and purpose is One Thing Only: to glorify God and to enjoy God's presence forevermore? This in itself implies the existence of *Zoe,* and the existence of the soul.

I recently heard one famous singer quote another in saying, "You need to do something for your career every day." Well, it could also be said that we need to seek food for our soul every day. The difference between this pursuit and the natural (and often bloody) instincts that drive the food-chain, is that benefit moves both in and out of the soul.

As we nurture the life within us, we have more with which to feed others. As Jane Regan, a volunteer of the Minnesota Council of Churches said, "I learned about affluence. After sharing my food, I am not thinner. After sharing my plants, I still have too many. After sharing my resources, I am not poor. After sharing my life, I am much richer."

Mere Christianity (New York: Macmillan, 1943), p. 139.

Blessings and Butterflies

May God kindle in me the fire of love to bring me
alive and give warmth to the world.
Lead me from death to life, from falsehood to truth.
Lead me from despair to hope, from fear to trust;
Lead me from hate to love, from war to peace.
Let peace fill my heart, the world, the universe . . .
—A New Zealand Prayer Book (1997)

Try saying this silently to everyone and everything you see
for thirty days and see what happens to your own soul:
"I wish you happiness now and
whatever will bring happiness to you in the future."
If we said it to the sky, we would have to stop polluting;
if we said it when we see the ponds and lakes and streams,
we would have to stop using them as garbage dumps and
sewers; if we said it to small children we would have to
stop abusing them, even in the name of training; if we said
it to people, we would have to stop stoking the fires of
enmity around us. Beauty and human warmth would take
root in us like a clear, hot June day. We would change.

—Joan Chittister,
In a High Spiritual Season

Chapter Six

*A*ny moment of prayer—of blessing ourselves and others—is by definition a "soul moment."

There is new scientific evidence, according to Paul Pearsall, Ph.D., in his book *The Heart's Code*, that the heart itself holds the key to our soul. Not just the sentimental idea of our "heart" that we give as a valentine to our lover—but our real, beating, pulsing, blood-pumping organ. In fact, the heart, according to Dr. Pearsall, has its own form of intelligence.

Our heart, he writes, both receives and exudes a special kind of energy, and facilitates a storing of information within all the cells of the body. He points out that what we call the soul is at least in part the sum total of these cellular memories. The soul can be described as *the effect that who we are*, deep within, *has* on our total being, including our physical makeup.

He proposes that we in the West have been too brain-focused in our approach to information and communication. Rather, he says, we should pay attention to what our hearts are constantly telling us, and how our hearts may even, with every beat, be sending out subtle signals to other souls, in a network of blessing—or curse.

Blessing others begins in our hearts—apparently, both physically and spiritually. The ancient wisdom that saw the heart as the seat of the emotions was not merely metaphorical, according to Dr. Pearsall.

If this is true, then prayer for our hearts to be open to God, to be open to peace (as in the lovely prayer from the *New Zealand Prayer Book,* quoted at the beginning) literally *can* lead to peace filling up the world, the universe.

Jesus said to *Bless, and curse not.* When we send words out into the world—even angry words directed at other motorists in their insulated cars, who can't hear us (I gently remind my husband)—it still matters. And conversely, when we consciously seek to love our enemies rather than curse them, no matter what they have done to us—*something is changed in the universe.*

It is like the "butterfly effect." It is said that a butterfly fluttering its wings in Africa can cause an avalanche in the Alps. *Love's* avalanche can start with as small a movement as the stirring of our heart toward someone else, in forgiveness and compassion. Madeleine L'Engle once likened forgiveness to a little goldfish wiggling its tail. Not much measurable life there, but enough to indicate that there is hope. . . . Even the slightest movement toward God or the other person can always grow and swell into a heart full of love— and healing.

How does anything wonderful begin? We need whimsical examples, sometimes, to wake us up to the very simplest truths. A child knows that a smile can work wonders. Sometimes we have forgotten, and our fixed, worried adult expressions simply engender more tension and create more separations between us in the world.

The author J. M. Barrie, Peter Pan's creator, must have known something about the power of blessing (not to mention, flying). He has his famous forever-child Peter Pan say: "When the first baby laughed for the first time, the laugh broke into a thousand pieces and they all went skipping about, and that was the beginning of fairies." Can you think of a better explanation? A butterfly, a goldfish, a child's laugh . . . who can estimate their power?

Consider some of the rhetorical questions that God asks of Job in the Old Testament. Notice the playfulness, the whimsy, the profundity of these probing queries:

"Has the rain a father, or who has begotten the drops of dew? . . . Can you bind the chains of the Pleiades, or loose the cords of Orion? . . . Who has the wisdom to number the clouds?"[1]

If we had answers to these questions, if we had been there when God set it all in motion, then maybe we, smug in our souls, could stand above it all and pass judgments on other people and the world. But who qualifies? Job certainly realized that he didn't. He answered, "I know that you, God, can do all things, and that no purpose of your can be thwarted."[2] This is the God who backs up our blessings, just as gold used to stand behind our dollar bills.

It is the God of the butterfly and the dewdrops and the stars who also connects us as souls to each other and to all of creation. In blessing ourselves, in blessing others, we are merely tapping into that source through words that are timely, and spirits that, we hope, fit our words. God does the rest!

How freeing it is to know that we don't have to solve all the potential problems facing us in the new millennium—at least not today. Most of us spend our lives spinning in the circles of busyness and striving. Yes, there is a time and a place for every activity and work under the sun. But what most of us are lacking—and long for desperately—is a spirit of deep soul-surrender to God, and the ability to bless all other living creatures. To bless, and curse not.

And so, let us bless others in everyday life—to help us learn our finger exercises, our "scales," so to speak. When you bless, *use words of Scripture*, or your own words, or beautiful phrases you come across in your reading. *Learn to bless,* and *spread the blessing.* Learn to laugh: as Reinhold Niebuhr said, "Humor is a prelude to faith and laughter is the beginning of prayer."

Butterflies . . . energy exuding from the heart . . . and laughter itself that seems to have wings . . . Somehow I see these gifts as wonderful, true pictures that can teach us how to live as souls before our God. And, as always, we must begin as we are, where we are right now.

Leslie Weatherhead wrote this fitting prayer for souls who seek to bless:

"Lord, come in this quiet moment of meditation; call me again, lead me in your way for me, let the assurance of your friendship take away my fears. Let every shadow make me look up into your blessed face. Let me rise up now and follow you."

[1]Job 38:28, 31, 37a.
[2]Job 42:2.

Precious Cargo

Why have this treasure in earthen vessels . . .

—2 Corinthians 4:7

. . . how frugal is the chariot
That bears a human soul!
—Emily Dickinson

Chapter Seven

Sometimes the most ordinary events can cause us to "stop, look, and listen" for soul-meaning.

It is a perfect late October afternoon in the southeast. It could be summer but for the slight mustiness in the air from already-fallen leaves, a certain cast of light through trees that are beginning to wear their seasonal camouflage. The elementary and junior high schools have been dismissed early (at least, children with parents who can pick them up at noon; the rest stay on to drudge and watch the clock in half-empty classrooms).

It is Homecoming for the local high school, and the annual parade of queen and court, marching band and attendant floats, pick-up trucks, police cars and hangers-on . . .

How could I refuse to join the party . . . when my daughters asked me to write appropriate notes to whisk them both—as well as heart-daughter Cassi—away from the mundane, to the edge of enchantment?

Oh, it is just a gaggle of lovely southern belles playing at Hollywood—each girl with her stiffly-suited escort waving to us gawkers from the back of a flatbed or (if lucky) an open convertible. The wrapped pieces of candy thrown from slowly passing parade cars is not stardust. The sun shines brightly on backyard-constructed, crepe-paper-smothered floats and lop-sided victory signs.

True, when the smartly blue-uniformed brass band works its way to where our car is parked at the Amoco station, the strains of "I Wish I Were in Dixie" strike me with an unexpected poignancy. There is a wakeup realization that we ARE in Dixie, sane and sound, where it seems my children have grown like Topsy . . . from toddlers to teenagers in the whiff of a breath of mere years.

This is home to us, through the effects of strings we ourselves didn't pull, graces that have met us head-on and rendered us securely rooted in place and time, blessed with "a local habitation and a name . . . " Winchester, Tennessee, hometown of Dinah Shore . . . stomping ground of David (we don't say Davy) Crockett . . . and home to Sir John Templeton.

These young women who sit beside me on the bumper and hood of the car, the milling crowd of adults and children of all sizes, aspirations, and backgrounds . . . not to mention the stars of the parade—who are important enough for us to come and admire for their fifteen minutes of fame—*all bear precious souls*—NO—they *are* precious souls. Not one misses a step, but the Heavenly Father sees, and cares.

I see other mothers I have met in earlier years, their sons (and sometimes daughters) now towering over them like giants looking down at earthlings. Could these aliens be the cute toddlers they once had in tow? At the junior high I sometimes feel dwarfed (at 5' 4") by football players. Time marches on.

Like many parents here in the Bible Belt, I have prayed on the run through the lunch-packing and the bus field trips . . . the morning commute and the unexpected "snow" days . . . the church Christmas pageants and the dance recitals. Ruminating about the precious souls in my care—yes, of course. But the love, the underlying care, has been a backdrop, a muted theme, yet a sustained note that has gotten us through ear infections and broken glasses and bouts of mono . . . through honors and band concerts and late-night scrambles to find posterboard. It, not cotton, is the fabric of our lives.

The precious cargo each of us bears is hidden, the fragile spirit of a developing person, rubbing shoulders against other mortals and seeking some kind of traffic direction to know where to be next, how to act, what to accomplish in the compression of time. Somehow, I have heard, and do believe, that children's souls develop best in the tug and fray of our own ordered (and occasionally dysfunctional) lives of adult grappling and coming-to-terms with the realities of existence.

Here we are, not on parade ourselves . . . but vicariously processing toward something. Life surely is moving on . . . next year Sarah will don one of those very band outfits and add the sounds of her trombone to the mix. She looks on with special interest, sizing up the stance and sound of these rhythmic pilgrims.

One song that was sometimes included in the girls' dance recitals always made me cry. "Turn around . . . Where are you going, Little One?" First they're three, then four, then grown—taller than you—and waving to you as they blithely go out your door. Can drivers licenses be far ahead?

Enough! On this warm, leisurely afternoon they want soft drinks. They want to stop at the library. Dinner is simmering at home in the crockpot. I've folded up my work for the day with little resistance. A day like this calls for an act of renunciation to fully enjoy the here-and-nowness of our souls together, just as we are at this juncture in time.

Just a bunch of people . . . southerners and some of us northern transplants . . . but all of us cherished and nurtured by the Lover of souls who created us. What purposes lie ahead for these young people? No one can tell. We do what we can, encourage gifts and honor achievements, help them work on weaknesses—and love unconditionally, as love has been showered on us.

The girls hop in—precious cargo filling my car. I carefully maneuver out of the non-parking space, and we are on our way. The parade is a memory, except for some distant pounding footsteps. Ordinary life, in all its fullness, its frustrating particularity, takes up where it never left off.

Emily Dickinson was really speaking of books not parades: "no frigate like a book . . . This traverse may the poorest take/Without oppress of toll:/How frugal is the chariot/That bears a human soul!" But it speaks to me of this everyday traverse of simply doing the next thing. We walk lightly with souls, our own and others'. But what chariot can compare to the bearing and shape of one's beloved child, a now-and-future manifestation of embodied love?

The Dirty Pastry

. . . what is sown is perishable, what is raised
is imperishable . . .

—1 Corinthians 15:42

To you it has been given to know the secrets
of the kingdom of heaven . . .

—Matthew 13:11

For the hour to reap has come...
—Revelation 14:15

Chapter Eight

$\mathcal{A}$ couple of years ago my husband planted some fig trees in our front yard, well knowing that we wouldn't enjoy their fruit any time in the near future. We were actually just pleased to have found a variety of fig that purportedly could withstand a Tennessee winter (with some precautionary cover during freezes).

Then, to our surprise, this spring one of the fledgling trees bore us a total of three edible figs. We washed them and gleefully ate them on the spot. True, they weren't the most succulent samples—but we enjoyed the treat, seeing them as harbingers of future harvests, a sign of hope.

I have always loved fresh figs—a rare, elusive taste when one grows up in suburban Chicago. I learned early that the plump, fleshy ripe figs that grew on my grandmother's trees in Gulfport, Mississippi, were a delight for savoring only in season, when one was visiting that Mecca of the South.

ISABEL ANDERS

She could and did send us generous bags and boxes of pecans from her backyard trees—enough for baking Christmas cookies and nut breads through the year. But those perishable figs, with their juicy pulp and edible, crunchy seeds, that were "better than candy" when caught at their peak—these could not be mailed. They had to be savored in the moment.

Some things can be stored for later—others can't.

Jesus used the fig tree as an example of fruitfulness and barrenness in several of his stories or parables. It is a natural symbol of bringing to fullness, offering reward, promising bounty. Although the fig was more of a staple in a desert climate (while it is a delicacy to us), I enjoy the whimsical thought that the experience of this delectable fruit might even be granted us in heaven, in seasonless availability.

While eating and drinking, streets of gold, a tree of life, and a flowing river are "mere" pictures of what heaven might offer, they do help us grasp at truths of the soul. For instance, I heard this modern parable of "The Dirty Pastry" a few years ago, and its poignancy has stuck with me:

A man who had been fabulously rich and powerful in his life on earth woke up and found himself in a small, dark room. He felt it had to be some mistake. Then he remembered the operation, the pain, the floating away from the table . . . the silence and the blackness.

He shook himself awake. Surely, no matter where he had ended up in the afterlife, there would be some provision! He rang a small bell that lay by his side. Sure enough, a steward came to his door, bearing a covered platter. His stomach growled as he greedily lifted the top. There, on a plain, rough board, lay one dirty pastry, smashed on one side and sprinkled with soot.

"Ugh!" he muttered. "Where's my meal? Is this some kind of joke?"

The steward merely nodded and left silently.

Sighing, the man brushed off the pastry, made the best of it, and lay back down for another dark interval.

The next day it was the same thing. The bell . . . the steward . . . the ceremoniously served dirty pastry!

"What's going on here?" he shouted. "I demand to see a menu! What nerve! Do you know who I am?"

"Yes, indeed," answered the stoic steward. "You are the man who, in his lifetime, always made sure that his own needs were met. You were stingy—with family, friends, servants. In fact, that made it difficult for us to prepare for you. Do you remember that last banquet, when a poor man knocked at your door? He begged for food, but you didn't find it in your heart to have him fed in the kitchen. No, you just tossed him one meager pastry that had been dropped and stepped on. It is that very fare that you yourself are now being served. It is all you gave us to work with. It's only what you give away that lasts, you know . . . "

For this man, like the rich man in the story of Lazarus the beggar, it was too late. His barns and houses back on earth may have been full. But his store of generosity was empty.

It's relatively easy to give away what we don't need or value anyway. But this parable says to me that nurturing our own soul necessarily involves caring for others. It is in self-forgetfulness, when we are simply planting and sowing and building and saving and restoring for those who will reap after us . . . that we reflect something of the economy of heaven.

Recently I read about a disturbing new book that proposes a radical approach to work and financial planning. Don't follow your bliss, it advises. . . . Don't do what you love, expecting that compensation and fulfillment will follow. Rather, the authors say (with unembarrassed candor), *just live for money,* put yourself first, feather your own nest, do anything you have to do to save and invest and make it grow during your productive years so that you can retire rich and do whatever *you* want. *That's success,* they blithely assert.

I came of age in the sixties when (no matter how we today view the results) ideals still lived. My generation wanted to make a difference in the world. The greedy eighties were still ahead. Some of us by then had already chosen our paths of vocation and never looked back. We had decided what was of value, and like permanent programming, it stuck in our consciousness. I wanted *fulfillment,* which seemed to be: to know and do (and spread) the truth, as much of it as I would be allowed to handle.

Don't do good, don't live for ideals, don't bother helping others, become a money machine? Is anybody actually buying into this new philosophy? It occurs to me that if a picture of the dirty pastry were emblazoned on the glossy cover of this new book, it might serve as a warning about where this kind of thinking can lead.

Sure, it's allegory. The soul is slippery, remember, hard to describe, to catch, to pin down or picture in any way but a cartoon exaggeration. British writer W. Somerset Maugham once wrote that in good literature the characters are "not lit by the hard light of common day but suffused in a mysterious grayness. . . . It is their souls that you seem to see."

The characters presented to us in parables, for the good of our souls, appear to us in this way—not as fully fleshed-out beings, but as shades and types of what can happen to the essence of the person in this life and beyond—based on the choices that we make here and now.

When the disciples asked Jesus why he spoke to them in parables, he answered, "To you it has been given to know the secrets of the kingdom of heaven, but to them it has not been given." They—the crowds, the nay-sayers, the skeptics—might hear the words. But they do not sink in. It takes a different set of eyes to see soulfully, to taste something of the harvest here on earth while we are in the midst of planting.

Remember the dirty pastry. *For to those who have, more will be given, and they will have an abundance; but from those who have nothing, even what they have will be taken away.**

---

*Matthew 25:29.

The Weather
of the Soul

*You know how to interpret the appearance of the
sky, but you cannot interpret the signs of the times. . . .
Those who want to save their life will lose it, and
those who lose their life for my sake will find it. For
what will it profit them if they gain the whole world
but lose their own soul?*

—Jesus,
Matthew 16:3, 25-26

By wisdom a house is built, and by understanding it is established . . . Does not he who keeps watch over your soul know it? And will he not repay all according to their deeds?

—Proverbs 24:3,12

Chapter Nine

$\mathcal{I}$t's a battlefield out there. I'm not thinking of the world of business, or even of the many ongoing world battle-fronts. Rather, it seems that there is a lot more going on out in "space" than the word itself would imply.

I subscribe to a news service on my internet server that provides me with daily news articles containing key words that I picked when I set up the selection process. I chose the word "space" because it keeps me aware of explorative technology and theories that are on the cutting edge of discovery—daily. Of course, the imperfect system also sends me articles on parking-lot spaces and space heaters and such. But those articles are easily jettisoned into the cybertrash.

Late last year I received a science report: "New Tool Helps Predict Space Storms." Now that we have extended the borders of (temporarily) habitable human abodes to include orbiting spacecraft, we have astronauts who must continually take heed of "space weather." A new instrument, called a "coronograph," lodged aboard the SOHO spacecraft and jointly operated by NASA and the European Space Agency, aids the technical accuracy in predicting the hazards known as "space storms." These tempests in the celestial stewpot can threaten the courses of astronauts in orbit, and knock out power and communication systems on earth as well.

The "coronograph" enables scientists to detect solar eruptions, or "coronal mass ejections"—blasts that actually throw huge chunks of the sun's atmosphere toward earth. Nine such eruptions were detected in the first half of last year. One permanently knocked out a major communications satellite, Telstar 402. The success rate of the new instrument can serve to make the weather in space more predictable and allow scientists to better protect our investment in space "real estate."

What next? We are developing telescopes and cameras to explore the farthest reaches of the known universe. More sophisticated detectors aid those scientists concerned about the dangers of asteroids colliding with earth. Soon, asking "What's the weather in space?" might be as relevant as "Do I need a jacket today?"

From what I have seen on television and read in the papers and through my internet service over the past few years, I have no doubt that we will continue to extend our knowledge out into the universe—and keep probing into the minute mysteries of cellular biology as well—until we are eventually able to ask someone about the "weather" occurring in any measurable space.

But what about the weather of the soul? Where, for that matter, *is* the soul? How can we tap its resources and harness its energy? predict its reactions . . . measure its depths . . . or correct its "defects" in time?

It is a curious truth that we won't find our soul by directly looking for it. If we would discover ourselves, and know our souls, the Bible tells us, we must first seek God. Wisdom is the way to building up the house of the soul, and to living in "rooms" filled with the knowledge that the Book of Proverbs likens to "precious and pleasant riches."

God is the one who knows us in our inward parts, and communes with our innermost beings. To Martin Luther, the soul's aim was to have "God deep in the flesh." We read the Gospels not so much to "find" treasure as *to be found ourselves,* and to discover how much we are treasured by God. Our souls are themselves the *pearl of great price* that God knows and loves and cultivates and redeems.

We can read the Psalms as a mirror of the soul, a reflection of the weather of doubt and fear and death— and God's answers to the ancient poet(s), promising joy and restoration and peace and life everlasting. Approaching the Bible, however, one might heed the warning: *Rough weather ahead!* This journey is not for the faint-hearted, the weak-souled. But the sustenance that will be provided is genuine meat and drink; or, to change the metaphor, amazing healing and calming of our troubled waters.

The secret and the key is that we can't really experience this until we willingly enter in.

For God alone my soul waits in silence;
from him comes my salvation.[1]

O that I had wings like a dove!
I would fly away and be at rest . . .
I would hurry to find a shelter for myself
from the raging wind and tempest . . . .[2]

You are my Father, my God, and the Rock of my
salvation![3]

My soul is satisfied as with a rich feast,
and my mouth praises you with joyful lips . . .[4]

[1]Psalm 62.
[2]Psalm 55:6-8.
[3]Psalm 89:26.
[4]Psalm 63.

The Ladder and
the Dance

*Somehow I have to trust that God is at work in me
and that the way I am being moved to new inner and
outer places is part of a larger movement of which I
am only a very small part.*

—Henri Nouwen

Then Jacob dreamed, and behold, a ladder was set up on the earth, and its top reached to heaven; and there the angels of God were ascending and descending on it. And he called the name of that place Bethel.

—Genesis 28:12

Chapter Ten

I know about places where—like Jacob's ladder—heaven "touches" earth. One such place comes to mind immediately—and it is not a church. Rather, it is an amazing spread-out school (a former high school campus) boasting a cluster of classrooms that serves our county as a kind of mega-kindergarten. All the children who go there are the same age, just entering elementary school. What a concept! Everything is neatly geared to their size, their interests—from the placement of the lockers to the original, colorful artwork that adorns the hallways (painted by local artists).

All the teachers specialize in guiding first steps toward education. The playground is just the right size for small limbs. There are no big bullies to deal with. But those facts are actually *not* why I think of heaven in connection with Townsend School.

When we first came to Middle Tennessee, my older daughter had left behind a beautiful private school in

Ohio where, in pre-kindergarten (as it was called) she had begun to learn "socialization." How, I wondered, would she fare in a public school setting?

As there were no other options, I prayed falteringly for the best. I had many other more pressing concerns, and larger decisions to be made. If God had brought us here, as we believed, then this county's schools would have to "work" for us too.

No sooner had I walked into the gymnasium to register her, than a lovely, dignified dark-haired woman who seemed to be in charge singled us out, gently routed us toward her own line of registrants, and, pointing to my daughter, told another teacher, "I'll take this one."

I didn't see any flashes of light (other than generous beams of sunlight cast through open windows above the bleachers) or hear voices (except for the chattering of mothers and the occasional father with children in tow). But I know now beyond a doubt that angels were present, guiding us through a school registration line as surely as a compass points a wayfarer home.

Mary Ruth, who turned out to be both the principal of the school and one of its classroom teachers, proved to be not only the ideal teacher and most loving Christian example for my daughter; she also became my soul-friend—and is a close and loving confidante up to this very day, in a bond that only grows stronger each year.

I might as well have been wandering in the wilderness, for all I could have articulated what we *really* needed, or even, specifically, what to ask God for. But none of that mattered. The angels were there—hidden perhaps, in the dust-speckled sunlight . . . or hiding in the rafters. There is no doubt.

What is sure is that *that spot*, on a weathered hardwood gym floor, in front of a wooden table stacked with registration cards, became a "Bethel," a place from which I could never again doubt God's love and care (except for moments when, in human weakness, I momentarily forget).

The Old Testament figure of Jacob was a wanderer too. His aged father Israel had sent him away from his native Canaan to go and find a wife in the home of his uncle, Laban. In his dream, as his head lay upon a stone, he was granted in advance by God the very land on which he was lying, for himself and his descendants. Not only this, but no matter how far they would wander from this place where "heaven touched earth," God would bring them back to this land.

When Jacob awoke, he said, "Surely the Lord is in this place. This is none other than the house of God . . . the Gate of Heaven!"* This spot he named Bethel, and there he made a vow that if God would provide for him and bring him back to his father's house in peace, he would render back a tenth of everything to God. This was consecration.

I wish I could say that I had that much understanding in the middle of a hot Southern afternoon and a mix of emotions as my firstborn started kindergarten. But I knew no more than to venture the next step, answer the necessary questions, take my daughter by the hand, go and buy the required school supplies—and trust God for the outcome.

But now, looking back, I have gained perspective and can affirm with joy, "How awesome was that place! Surely heaven touched earth, and we were surrounded by mercy and grace, flowing out and running over . . . "

My soul is ever a wanderer, despite what my rational mind thinks it is planning and performing. I rely on God to remind me of these Bethels, to instruct me in my own dependence and weakness so that I will always remember that *it was God and not I* who has brought forth beauty from ashes . . . and has allowed so much joy in the paths of love and service that have been granted during this last decade of my life.

Through no coincidence, I'm sure, Mary Ruth was with me on another pivotal day about a year after we met. We were having lunch at the only castle in town—literally a castle, turned into a restaurant. In fact, it was the last time anyone had lunch there—as it burned to the ground under unknown circumstances later that night. But that is another story.

At that hour we were simply present to each other, thankful for the gift of unexpected, growing friendship and soul-sharing that had been granted us. I was seeking more secure employment as an editor. And through her suggestion and a chain of people and circumstances I could not have imagined in my wildest dreams—much less orchestrated—I made contact with a publisher who was looking immediately for someone with just my background and skills. While two pilgrims, she and I, were gathered together in active praying, angels were hovering, plans in hands. It took a trip up a (literal) mountain, a string of "chance" encounters—and soon I was launched into my new vocation.

I have told my children that there are places where heaven touches earth—and that we can expect them to be revealed to us at times. "We are climbing Jacob's ladder, soldiers of the cross." The image of the ladder has been a popular one in classical spirituality, as it offers a scale of height, suggesting a dazzling up-and-down movement to which our souls can aspire. Sometimes we need to look back to "measure" our progress.

But I think also of C. S. Lewis's fitting image of the *dance of all creation,* in which we are simply following the steps of the moment, as they are revealed to us . . . finding our place as we can, unable at any time to view the design of the whole for the effort of our own particular movements. The Dance speaks to me too of a heavenly ordering of our earthly journeys.

I am content *not* to see the glory of it all, sweeping above and about us, except as God wills. It is enough to move trustingly in place, to sit one out when required, to have my dance card filled as it is given. But I do believe also that sometimes we are graciously brought back to the land—the place, physically, where, for us, a miracle occurred. Our souls need touch with tangible reality, a chance to mark a spot—even on a foot-worn gymnasium floor—in order to affirm that *where we stood is,* in a mystery, *the "house" of God, the "gate of heaven."*

*Genesis 28:17.

A Distant Mirror

*And the Word became flesh and lived among us,
and we have seen his glory, the glory as of a
father's only son, full of grace and truth.*

—John 1:14

There are two ways of spreading light:
to be the candle or the mirror that reflects it.
—Edith Wharton

Chapter Eleven

*I*n my morning devotional time I have been reading of Hildegard of Bingen, born the tenth child to a noble family in the Rhineland in 1098. Hildegard had memories—not just from childhood, but from the time she was in her mother's womb—of strange visions seen with an inner eye. Images came to her, full of precise forms and colors, enlarging her soul through her eight decades of life.

Sometimes she speaks of being taught directly by the Old Testament female figure, Sapienta, or Wisdom. This was not just a vague sense of being prodded by God—though the visions did have an admonitory authority. Rather, it was—in a time when women were taught to be quietly obedient and forbidden sometimes even to speak—indication that here indeed was *a light for God's people* in her own time.

Part of the instruction discerned by her was, in her middle age, to establish an autonomous community consisting of her small group of nuns—their own convent. As *magistra* of her community, she herself taught all the music for the Divine Office, writing text and music for antiphons, responsories, hymns, and sequences, plus the first extant sung morality play, based on a struggle pitting the devil against sixteen distinct female Virtues and their queen! During that time she also composed a complete herbal and a treatise on the causes and cures of a variety of illnesses.

This remarkable visionary and saint is the subject of a fictionalized biography, *Hildegard, the Last Year*, by Barbara Lachman[1], in which the author intersperses known events of Hildegard's life with extraordinary imaginings of Hildegard's inner thoughts during a period of enforced silence and trial at the very end of her days.

In a passage ruminating on her travels on the Rhine, to Wurzburg and Bamberg, Lachman creates these thoughts for Hildegard: "Up and down, north and south, climbing on this great tree of a river, and on to its contributing rivers. It was as if the Rhine led us [Hildegard and her party on her preaching tours] through a vast bloodworks feeding a body of monasteries and cathedrals, and I always returning at last, exhausted, to the beauty of the valley of the Nahe, our own vein of the Rhine. . . . I began at that time to have visions of the human body as it corresponds, part for part, to the entire cosmos. Our bodies and the mystery of Christ interpenetrating one another with the constant modulation of the four elements."

For Hildegard (for these images are consistent with her actual writings), *Christ had come,* imaging forth the Almighty God, not only in the flesh and blood of her nuns and all ministers, but *in all flesh*—indeed, in all creation. "I became part of the waterway somehow connecting people to Christ's faraway limbs, instilling in them a hunger for the real source and a discernment forswearing the substitutes that are offered."

In the diary-like chapters of this remarkable book, there unfolds the story of an amazing soul: Through the stresses of unjust discipline (she and her nuns are given an interdict forbidding them to sing the Divine Office and to receive the Eucharist until they meet a demand that they cannot in good conscience comply with) . . . Hildegard remains resolute and focused. To me Hildegard's example is reminiscent of the way of light expressed in the Prologue to the Gospel of John: *The light shines in the darkness, and the darkness did not overcome it.* Hildegard testified to that light in a world darkened by violence and schism, ambition and peril. In short, a day and time not unlike our own.

For instance, she wrote:

"I wonder sometimes whether I am alone in needing to see *all* of the created universe interrelated. . . . Wisdom has brought me further elucidations of divine mysteries in our own time . . . and connections between parts of the human body and those of the universe. . . . I must see the shape of the cosmos as it is progressively revealed to me, for it has changed from its stratified egg shape to that of an orb pierced by the Godhead."

This sort of "cosmic egg" picture can be seen as Hildegard's version of the mystery of the Incarnation. And it is, of course, also the principal image of the means of Jesus' human birth—the piercing of an egg by God, bringing forth the God-man, "full of grace and truth." In her visionary experience, that which is abstract and otherworldly and ineffable comes down to the simplest of diagrams—accessible to us today. *Jesus Christ, born of a virgin, God's only Son, from the bosom of the Father's heart, made known—even to us . . .*

This is but a glimpse of the soul-wisdom of an ancient personage, whose life was a mirror of Jesus' Incarnation: an embodiment in her time and place of the mysteries of God at work in the universe. But if our own souls also can be said to mirror that reality, then perhaps we can be as bold as Hildegard in our words and actions.

In a recent edition of the *Huntsville* (Alabama) *Times,* I read about some modern iconoclastic women—with a nineties twist. These women are nuns too, and they seek to express the Incarnation in their midst as they believe they have been led to in their own time. But silence and obedience are not their chosen approach—at least not as regards official Catholic policy.

"It started with a group of religious women getting together for a meal. They blessed the food. They prayed. They talked about how good it made them feel to be together with God. . . . And then they did something they believed could get them excommunicated. They held a Eucharist without a priest. Their actions are being replayed over and over, often in secret, in communities across the country." The article estimates that at least a thousand such groups now exist. Most are small gatherings of fewer than thirty.

They haven't left their home parishes—WomenEucharist, as they call it, is supplementary. And, perhaps as a sign of gradually softening attitudes, Church officials generally have reacted mildly. "Although many U. S. Catholic women are disenchanted with the Church's stance on matters of gender . . . most are disengaging, not protesting." Says one spokeswoman, Sister Donna Quinn, "We'd like women across the country to continue to light these fires. We call it a liturgy. If women think of this as Eucharist, it is; and if they do not think of it as Eucharist, it isn't. I think it's in the heart of the women who participate."[2]

What is the real picture here? Perhaps you could call it simply some souls' "picnic" with their God. Jesus made the practice work on a number of occasions—without setting three forks and linen napkins at each place-setting. Sister Beth Rindler tells how, when she first blessed the bread and wine, it felt wrong. "Then I thought, Jesus gave the bread and wine to everybody. So why not?"

[1]Boston: Shambhala Publications, 1997.
[2]*The Huntsville Times*, Sept. 12, 1998.

Soul Questions

The dead man came out, his hands and feet bound with strips of cloth, and his face wrapped in a linen cloth.

—John 11:44

One item about the Resurrection of Jesus has sometimes been overlooked: Jesus showed Himself after death only to those who loved Him.

—George A. Buttrick

Chapter Twelve

*A*mong our questions about the soul, a good one to ask would be:

"What do you think happened to Lazarus after he rose from the dead?"

"What?"

"I've been thinking about it. We don't know, do we? And it's the question. Whatever do you think the Gospel writers were dreaming about not to finish the story?"

The above dialogue is from Sophie Burnham's *(A Book of Angels)* fascinating novel, *Revelations.*[1] The comments and questions about the New Testament story of Jesus' raising of Lazarus are initiated by an Episcopal priest, Tom Buckford, who has had some unusual experiences of glory and revelation (or was it madness?) himself.

"Isn't rising from the dead important?" asks his friend and vestryman John Woods.

Tom answers that no modern journalist would stop the story there. Here's the only man on earth brought back to life . . . of course they'd all rush in for his testimony, holding out microphones to ask, "Mr. Lazarus. How're you feeling? Can you tell us what it was like on the other side? . . . "

Here was a man who'd seen God! He was living in the Light. He was bathed in "the music of eternal silence," and then thrown back into his physical body. And what about the body? For three days it has been *buried*. "Is he cured of that wet-rot? We aren't told."

Woods replies that we'd have to assume he was. "Christ wouldn't leave him in a worm-eaten body." . . . Or maybe he came back healed in every way, having experienced a dimension in which he no longer had to see reality as polarized duality—either/or. Maybe he was alive on another level, knowing through dramatic experience that there *is no death.* . . . "Maybe he was alive with a quickening of the soul that most of us never know."

Could he have been "born again"? Suppose we've got the whole thing wrong, the novel teases us to consider: and we're only alive *after* we die. Suppose Lazarus was brought back here to earth—from *life?*

Sometimes I, too, wonder if we've even got the question right. Lately there seems to be endless discussion of the nature of human life and death. Are we bodies? Or bodies and souls? Does the body die and the soul live on? Don't we, with this language, risk falling into the same old either/or dualism that Christianity rejects?

Yet how can we begin to ask the right soul questions?

The highly popular Indian doctor Deepak Chopra asserts that the following five "realizations" are expressed in every spiritual tradition as a core of spirituality:

1. I am spirit.

2. This moment is as it should be.

3. Uncertainty [possibility?] is part of the overall order of things.

4. Change is infused with non-change ("Life is an eternal dance").

5. Entropy (the principle of the degradation or disorganization of matter and energy) holds no threat because it is under the control of *infinite organizing power* (emphasis mine).[2]

While Dr. Chopra's philosophy stops short of an Incarnational perspective (matter is seen as pure projection); and I fail to find in it enough ethical guidance or acknowledgment of the role of evil . . . still there is much truth in these "realizations." *More than matter matters.*

Yet British theologian Helen Oppenheimer, I believe, speaks more helpfully to us in our "Lazarus dilemma." In her excellent book, *The Hope of Heaven*,[3] she offers us many dimensions to consider in her extended argument against the old language of dualism (soul/body). She writes of resurrection:

"Christians are apt to suppose that the answer [to such questions] is a sturdy reaffirmation of immortal souls. But surely Christians ought to put their hopes, not in 'souls' but in God. Instead of pinning our faith to immortality as a possession of ours, we trust, much more coherently, in the power and mercy of God. The Creator who made us can remake us without needing to salvage our broken fragments."

So maybe our concerns about Lazarus' physical and/or spiritual experiences in and beyond the grave are really not the issue. Can we not rephrase the Question? Could not heaven and earth overlap? Isn't the important question, "Do you believe God never forsook him?" Oppenheimer quotes Austin Farrer in his work *Saving Belief*:

"'Space is a web of interactions between material energies which form a system by thus interacting. . . . Heaven can be as dimensional as it likes, without ever getting pulled into our spatial field, or having any possible contact with us of any physical kind. . . .'[4] How I wish we could explain Einsteinian theory to St. Augustine!"

So, *Where was Lazarus during that time "in the tomb"?* might be less relevant than where *we are* in relation to God right now. St. Augustine cried to God, "I realized that I was far away from Thee in the land of unlikeness . . . "*(Confessions)*. Perhaps we might come to the conclusion that—in any dimension of life or death—*God's presence is all that matters.*

How do we cultivate life during life? Surely our souls must learn to be receptive—we might say, to *awaken to love,* which transcends all dimensions.

Oppenheimer suggests that "the things we mind about on earth can be rehearsals for heaven, destined for fulfillment not for abandonment. It is still more to the point to say that the best rehearsal of all for heaven is to learn to delight in each other. If we find that we continue to do this by making and showing one another things, that is just what we should expect if we believe we are made in the image of God the Creator."

Forget the wet-rot and nightmares of the grave! Cannot the Creator of life also preserve life flawlessly? Perhaps the Gospel storytellers were not so lacking in their approach: Surely Lazarus' very reappearance in the body, and the hugs and reassurances that he was able to give his loved ones around him, said it all.

[1]*Revelations*, Sophie Burnham, (New York: Ballantine Books, 1992).

[2]*Ageless Body, Timeless Mind*, (New York: Harmony Books, 1993), pp. 169, 144.

[3]Cambridge, Mass.: Cowley, 1988, p. 83.

[4] Hodder & Stoughton, 1964.

Life at the Edges

Darkness may be creative, for it is there that
God plants seeds to grow and bulbs to flower. It is at
night that the sheep that are scattered are gathered
into the sheepfold, when the children come home to
their mother, and the soul back again to God.

—Fulton J. Sheen

Living is moving, time is a live creek bearing changing lights.
—Annie Dillard

Chapter Thirteen

$\mathcal{I}$ have a wonderful original black-and-white print by artist Joe DeVelasco hanging in our bedroom that has always spoken to me of the soul . . . and the edge of life as we know it.

Just below its center, a scribe (for me, it *has* to be John the Evangelist) writes (it must be the Revelation)—on a blank scroll. The long, sinewy strands of the prophet's hair—which form the suggested outlines of his body—also grow upwards into a kind of rope . . . or perhaps a tree, piercing a cloud, ingenuously separating the black fourth of the painting from the white three-fourths of its surface.

The Seer writes at the edge of Life and Death, Time and Eternity. Vague clouds and the body itself make the rip in time seem a mere coincidence. Eternity is here, now, "in the twinkling of an eye." Only art can convey so much with the few deft lines of a fine pen and the touches of a brush. I cherish this reminder that the soul is at home on the edges, having a "foot," so to speak, in both realities. Do not our dreams teach us this every night?

At this point in our collection of "soul moments" it seems hard to take inventory. What DO we really know about the soul (since all spiritual language must be somewhat metaphorical)? The painting . . . and the words of Scripture that speak of *a tree in Paradise* "for the healing of the nations" . . . say more to me than any catalogue one could compile of "things we can affirm about the soul."

I am always starting again at the beginning, seeking what I can affirm today of God's goodness in this moment, in the land of the living, as food for the journey. Saint Teresa spoke of "The Interior Castle," and of our way to God: "To make rapid progress and to reach the mansions we wish to enter, it is not so essential to think much as to love much: therefore you must practice whatever most excites you to this."

I sometimes practice thinking about how our lives touch the eternal here and now. Can we say of a "lucky break" or our best success that it furthers our progress toward those mansions awaiting us? Usually, we are in doubt. Although success may be extremely dangerous to the soul, so is failure. I find it more and more necessary to trust to God the mix of *all* the ups and downs of a day, a week, a year, a decade. Cannot the God of all creation manage to give us what we need in "the fullness of time"? I must always come back to trust. It is a battle of faith that never ends.

Yet, there is so much to do in the meantime. The duties of work and family life and parish and community sometimes give us little time to practice "balancing" on the edge. We feel as though we are rooted, grounded—as necessities bind us to the clock, the computer, the car. But the death of a loved one, a sudden catastrophe of nature (such as the ice storm that has just laid waste much of the Southeast right at Christmas this year) reminds us how fragile our lives really are.

Through Scripture, music, art, I am touching Eternity consciously for at least a few moments each day. The soul's other business in the land beyond the veil, across the thin black line, sometimes haunts my dreams. The Advent and Christmas Gregorian chants I have been listening to also keep my own pulsebeats in tune with the universal hum of life that underlies all reality. I have been reading David Steindl-Rast's wonderful book *The Music of Silence* about the spirituality behind the *Chant* recordings. His commentary on *Vigils* (the night watch hour) seems especially appropriate in this season:

Here is a quote (and why chant meets us in any condition):

"Vigils is an invitation to learn to 'trust in night,' to trust the darkness despite the immense fear it triggers. We have to learn to meet mystery with the courage that opens itself to life. Then we discover, as the Gospel of John puts it right in the prologue, 'The light shines in the darkness.' This doesn't mean that light shines *into* the darkness, like a flashlight shining into a dark tent. No, the good news that the Gospel of John proclaims is that the light shines right in the midst of darkness. A great revelation: the very darkness shines. . . .

"That is why the Psalmist sings: 'I will say to that darkness, be my light.' To recognize the darkness itself as light can be a great consolation. When we find ourselves in inner darkness, we cry out with the prophet, 'Watchman, what of the night?' . . . Listening deeply to chant, we will hear a darkness turned into sound, a darkness that shines."*

I especially love Advent, because we affirm through its dark days that the Light still shines. I like this too: "Contemplation literally means a continuous *putting together according to some measure.*" It is entering into another kind of "measuring" altogether. Steindl-Rast speaks of the hours being like "angels calling" to each other: "With this inner attitude, we will meet the angel of each hour and come to an understanding of the seeds the angel calls us to sow, the virtue the hour calls us to develop in our own lives."

Soul Moments

I love this writing (along with the music) because I feel, every day, that I'm trying to build some order out of chaos (life with teenagers)! But I have plenty of chaos in myself too. I need a sense of the hours flowing on this side of the Great Divide, so that on that Other Side the purpose of it all will become as crystal—and the excitement for the life of the soul that begins and swells on this side . . . will follow us into the Mansions that are prepared for us.

Alleluia!

[*]HarperSanFrancisco, 1995, p. 25.

"Nuns Fret Not"

Nuns fret not at their convent's
*   narrow room;*
And hermits are contented with
*   their cells . . .*
In truth the prison, unto which we doom
Ourselves, no prison is . . .

—William Wordsworth

O Lord, the house of my soul is narrow;
enlarge it that You may enter in.
—St. Augustine

Chapter Fourteen

*Y*esterday, the First Sunday After Christmas, we took a sort of "vacation" from our usual church service and went up to an 8:00 a. m. Eucharist at St. Mary's Convent. The drive there up the mountain took us past great patches of ice on the slopes that the sun had not yet reached.

After a winding drive into the woods, crunching our tires over branches in the road that the ice storm had felled, we saw the beloved modern structure of the convent finally coming into view. It was a bit foggy in the cold morning air, and the surrounding trees were still encased in crystal, like props from Fairyland.

St. Mary's is perched on a lookout point, and its windows have been designed to reveal from several sides the grandeur of the convent's setting. The chapel is small but airy, allowing light in from every side, and revealing to worshipers the beauty of the valley below. This very modern sanctuary, with its pillars and high round windows, at a glance could also be as ancient as one of the typical backdrops for the Annunciation—as seen in numerous Renaissance paintings.

"Small" and "limited" (though perhaps technically accurate) were the last thoughts I would use to describe this sacred space. Rather, the careful attention to detail, the simple but profound homily on John 1: "The Word became flesh . . . " and the generous hospitality we enjoyed made it as expansive an experience as any soul could desire.

We had a great time seeing old friends and meeting some new ones. As the morning warmed, the ice on the trees all started to melt, and afterwards, during the coffee hour, we looked out to the phenomenon of "raining" ice! Through all this natural and spiritual sustenance, my soul *did* magnify the Lord, and my spirit soared.

Of course, I do not live day to day in a narrow room; and I have perhaps more freedom in my work and daily life than many people. Yet as a searcher, I seek containment, focus, perspective, in order to know the exquisite joy of limitation for a purpose.

I once heard the author/guru Deepak Chopra giving lectures about the nature of reality/soul. He said people were always asking him how some could claim to have had out-of-body experiences—times when the soul would "fly" the narrow confines of the body and report great insights and adventures. He smiled his charming grin and changed the question, saying he always wondered *how did people manage to keep* their souls trapped in their bodies? That, to him, was a greater enigma.

It all depends on your understanding of soul, your conception of the vastness of the universe—of inner and outer "space" and its relationship to individual experience. The ancient Psalmist wrote, "Where can I go from your spirit? Or where can I flee from your presence? If I ascend to heaven, you are there; if I make my bed in hell, you are there. If I take the wings of the morning and settle at the farthest limits of the sea, even there your hand shall lead me . . . "* From where do these amazing flights of fancy come? Is it possible that it has *never* been unusual for some souls to see the "barriers" of time and space as fairly inconsequential?

We know from writings of many saints that their visions brought them "present" to the events of Christ's Passion—and sometimes even to creation itself. The Lady Julian of Norwich, England (ca. 1342–1420), speaks of God showing her "a little thing, the size of a hazelnut, lying in the palm of my hand, as round as a ball." She looked at it and thought, "What can this be?" And the answer was given, "All that was made." And she was also given to perceive that this nut, or ball of creation, was held in existence by Love—and God its Lover. It was not too small to be cherished and sustained in and by love.

Smallness, narrowness, is a relative thing—as is space. The Romantic poet Wordsworth wrote of the principle of "beauty within bounds" in his poem "Nuns Fret Not." In this sonnet he compared the chosen confinement of religious vocation to his own choice of the precisely defined strictures of the sonnet form itself. Since choosing to limit oneself for a purpose—for art, for God—*is* an act of beauty, he wrote, "hence for me / In sundry moods, 'twas pastime to be bound / Within the Sonnet's scanty plot of ground."

But he goes on to say: "Pleased if some Souls (for such there needs must be) / Who have left the weight of too much liberty, / Should find brief solace there, as I have found."

The weight of *too much* liberty? That is an almost incomprehensible thought to modern Western persons. Shouldn't our goal be to taste and experience and enjoy as much as possible?

Yet it is surely true that only by the artistic principle of "selection of detail" is anything worthwhile ever to be accomplished. Think of the artist with a canvas. Restricting? Of course. G. K. Chesterton once said that *the artist loves his limits; they constitute the thing he is working on.* It is by NOT painting the whole world (though Jack Frost seemed to have tried to do just that!) that one *concentrates* and produces beauty within measurable, heart-stopping bounds.

The Psalmist sometimes saw God as a rock, a refuge, a high tower—limited structures that bespeak safety and peace. And so, I find that also, within the essay of a thousand or so words, there is a way of saying—not everything—but *some* things that may remind us that *no soul can be considered too narrow when God deigns to dwell in it.*

*Psalm 139:7-10.

Soul-Friends

Great friendship is a delight:
a hyphen between two minds, a bridge between two wills.
—Elizabeth Selden

Anyone without a soul-friend is like a body
without a head.

—Ancient saying, quoted by
Thomas Cahill in *How
the Irish Saved
Civilization*

*When one has once fully entered into the realm of love,
the world—no matter how imperfect—becomes rich and
beautiful, for it consists solely of opportunities for love.*
                                        —Soren Kierkegaard

Chapter Fifteen

"You've got mail!"—who would have thought that a pleasant voice coming at you in your morning routine, right out of your computer, could be a sign of friendship? If friendship is a hyphen between two minds, our electronic media may be fast becoming the major means of connection between souls!

Time, distance, lack of visual/audio contact (except for those whose systems have such features) is beside the point. When a recent friend or an old one sends me immediate thoughts (sometimes we "chat" online in instant messages) there is real contact. "Reach out and touch someone" now often means reaching for a switch, hearing the reassuring hum of your machine warming up, and poising those fingers above the keyboard to send the signals down the line: *I've been thinking about you. Here's an idea, some information, or just a reminder that you're important to me, right in this moment* (as the time and date are electronically added to the message).

Now, not only are possibilities for friendship expanded—cyberspace itself becomes a potential medium for the transmittal of love. For friendship of the soul is, above all, an opportunity for affirming love and allowing it to grow before your very eyes.

Of course, some of us still communicate in the old ways as well—relying on "snail mail" when a clipping just must be sent, a card or gift carefully chosen and an enclosure included, or a package shipped. Sometimes we just have the need to hear another's voice over the line. In this "communicate, don't commute" age, we sometimes even take cross-country trips to experience real face-to-face encounter! The many choices for communication between souls can also showcase the many facets of love.

My children are growing up, with ease of soul, in the "global village"—just as was predicted by Marshall McLuhan, prophet of my undergraduate journalism school days. They take it for granted that we can be but a press of a button away from those we care about—or have just met, or have *any* connection to our life. Only the loss of electricity . . . or the loss of service of our internet provider (more often than we'd like) . . . can keep the wires of on-line friendship from staying warm.

Perhaps someday it will be necessary to teach a new generation the "history of friendship": how people managed to keep in touch before all this was possible! I remember, more than a decade ago, meeting for coffee with other young mothers, desperately trying to connect in some satisfying adult way while babies crawled around or blessedly snoozed in their strollers or had to be fed or changed around our staccato attempts at philosophical (or any meaningful) exchange.

It was exhausting just to try to stay connected to the adult world of friendship and spiritual sustenance. But we (most of us) survived and now find that our young adult children are soul-friends to us as well—when we can get their attention!

Friendship is, for me, another sign that the soul truly IS, and that we connect *as souls* when we touch the core of another's need, another's heart and mind. Most of my soul-friends (other than my father and my husband, whom I count right at the top) have been women. I could sing their names like a litany in any order: Marlene, Anita, Kathy, Mary Ruth, KiKi, Ruth, Patti, Myrna, Madeleine, Nancy, Dawn, Marianne, Susie, Katrelya, Debra, Chandler, Karen, LaVonne, Judy, Dandi, Jane, Katie, Theresa, Aida, Ellen, Jean, Basye, Linda, Fay, Elizabeth . . . and it is a flexible, growing melody. A few have already passed on to Eternity to a much-expanded world of love. And yet here, as in heaven, there is always room for another verse.

Although there are times when one particular soul-friend has just the ear you want and need at that moment, it seems that as we grow in love, the possibilities expand. Someone surprises us with a sort of grace-note: a book in the mail; a digital photograph of the last time we were together—suddenly on the screen; a phone call at a time of crucial need. It's easy to believe that soul-friends may be truly connected in ways more mystical than by cyberspace and phone lines.

Just as the saints can be for us mirrors of the glory of God, facets of the many virtues and qualities of Christ himself, teaching us about the journey all souls must take—so friends can be for us aspects of love, faces of most particular expression that together make up the whole unified, "peopled" kingdom of God.

For that reason, it is impossible to imagine heaven without visualizing the faces of those we love, and have loved, in our lifetimes. No wonder many souls have reported a kind of "life-review" in near-death or death experiences, in which beloved people were present to them, beckoning, inviting, accepting them unconditionally.

"Like the stars of the morning, they shine in their beauty . . . bright gems of his crown" went one chorus we sang as children. Who were these stars? "Little children, little children who love their Redeemer." And isn't that simple image surprisingly close to what we have been told in Revelation that our lives are to be about someday?

" . . . a multitude that no one could count, from every nation, from all tribes and peoples and languages, standing before the throne and before the Lamb, robed

in white, with palm branches in their hands . . . "[1]
"Blessing and honor and glory and might forever and
ever!"[2] Amen!

Then, truly, all moments are/will be but opportunities for love, before the throne of the One who is the
Lover of our souls.

[1]Revelation 7:9.
[2]Revelation 5:13.

"Ask Dad"

For God satisfies the longing soul,
and fills the hungry soul with goodness.

—Psalm 107:9

You never become truly spiritual by sitting down and wishing to become so. You must undertake something so great that you cannot accomplish it unaided.
—Phillips Brooks

Chapter Sixteen

*W*hen I was a little girl I truly thought that my father had the answer to any question—from mathematics to metaphysics. For one thing, he never failed to take my probings seriously, always making them a focus of interest, and engaging his own excellent mind . . . seeking a way to help me take the next step. Later, he guided me through the geometry that did not come naturally to me at all . . . and I introduced him to the space trilogy of C. S. Lewis, *Out of the Silent Planet*, *Perelandra*, and *That Hideous Strength*—paperbacks which we read in tandem and discussed endlessly.

I suppose it happened sometime in early college, when I was encountering areas of inquiry that he hadn't necessarily considered. It finally hit me that he was— not the seat of authority and wisdom I had supposed—but a "mere" searching soul too. Being an adult didn't mean that you understood it all. But he *did* set an example that showed me how to continue searching, trying new things, and, with God's help, discovering new strengths in my inner life for what might lie ahead.

Today when my children want some help related to grammar or syntax or literature, they come to me (since, as a veteran editor, I'm supposed to be something of a grammar expert). But when it comes to math or economics or political science or American (especially Confederate) history—then it is high time to "Ask Dad!"

My husband and I used to joke that between us we knew everything. But when one of us was asked a question, we'd say, "That's something *he* knows" or "That's one of the things *she* knows."

It was fine as long as the other party was unavailable for comment at the time. In reality, there is nothing wrong with not knowing something—if that very realization becomes a spur to seek and to ask and to find.

David Steindl-Rast writes in *The Music of Silence:* "A friend's young daughter said to him one morning, 'Dad, isn't it amazing that I exist?' Children know intuitively how surprising and delightful it is that there is anything at all. And the child in us never dies. We can lock it up, we can forget it, and we can neglect it badly, but it is still alive as long as we live. One of our great tasks is to liberate this child again, to encourage it to ask those deep questions children ask. Then we will look at everything through wondering eyes and receive everything with an open heart."[1]

I believe that this inquiring, child-spirit is very akin to the soul. It is the *questing continuity* within ourselves that keeps us "hungry" and "thirsty"—but that also reminds us there *is* a Source of fulfillment as long as we keep asking. God satisfies the longing soul, and continually refreshes, filling the empty, dry spirit with good things.

The German Dominican mystic Meister Eckhart (c. 1260—1327) gave us insight into what such a soul is like: "An empty spirit can do everything. What is an empty spirit? An empty spirit is one that is confused by nothing, attached to nothing, [nor] to any fixed way of acting, and has no concern whatever in anything for its own gain, for it is all sunk down into God's dearest will and has forsaken its own."

This is the sort of state that the philosopher Paul Ricoeur calls a "second naiveté"—that innocence that somehow endures on the *other* side of experience . . . that flourishes in the "not-knowing-but-seeking" soul. It is difficult to describe, but even more difficult to achieve.

In his fascinating book, *God: The Evidence,* Patrick Glynn writes about something like this "naiveté" in religious believers, who, "the argument might run . . . are too naive to understand how miserable life really is. Interestingly, there is a growing body of research showing that certain kinds of illusions are in fact conducive to happiness and also—what is perhaps more puzzling—to physical health and career success. In particular, the 'illusion' of optimism seems to be an important ingredient of a happy, healthy, and successful life."[2] He quotes psychologist Martin Seligman who writes: "Organized religion provides a belief that there is more good to life than meets the eye."

Is not this the very presumption of the seeking soul? The anthem of the Psalms? That God the Lord rewards those who seek, knock, ask? God teaches and preserves and encourages and delights and saves the very soul that longs for God as a deer pants after bubbling brooks.

The life of the soul is about journeying, seeking, searching, asking questions . . . but it is also about beginnings. My father, still humble and questing in his late seventies, told me on the phone recently, "You know, when it comes to praying I still feel like a beginner . . . " And in that spirit I remembered one reason he has been such an inspiration to me through the years. I said, "Then you are closer to truly praying than if you thought you really knew how." My heart leaped at the way God keeps our souls simple and close and comforted, rocked as though on a daddy's lap.

My younger daughter Emilie recently was asked to submit an essay for a book to be titled *Why Kids Believe in God*. She wrote:

I believe because God is. *I can't explain it any more than I can explain God himself. I just don't know how anyone can't. God has given me everything, so why shouldn't I give him everything I can?*

I believe in God because he gave up his Son for us. Because he loved us so much that he took away our sin. I'm reminded of him every time I open my eyes and look around.

When I was a little kid, I didn't really understand Christianity. All I knew were Bible stories and that every Sunday I went to Sunday School to wait for my mom to get out of church.

I guess the first time I actually understood it a little was one day when it was raining hard and my mom and I were alone at home. My sister was being driven home from a party and the streets were flooding. The electricity was off and we had lit some candles.

My mom and I got down on our knees and prayed. I suppose that was a very important moment in my life and I was only 5. I just know that God is there, and I believe.

I was incredibly touched by her recollection of drawing on faith, of seeking God and receiving assurance. I'm glad that she and I were, in that moment, beginners together. She, in her pure, unsullied perception, has tapped directly into the ontological argument for God and God's care for the soul. No philosopher can top that.

I am thankful for a family history of seekers and finders, of doers and thinkers who have contributed to my own faith. It is like a living chain of souls. The great theologian Phillips Brooks was once asked why he was a believer. He answered, "My aunt in Teaneck, New Jersey."

[1]p. 41.
[2]p. 73.

Sound Bites

*It is better to have a heart without words
than words without a heart.*

—John Bunyan

A desire realized is sweet to the soul.

—Proverbs 13:19

Chapter Seventeen

$\mathcal{I}$t seems that in the last couple of years the newest buzzword to make our ears prick up is "soul." Benefit to the "soul" is being claimed by a wide range of endeavors . . . everything from consuming certain hot cereals in the morning—to driving an especially safe model of car. Sometimes these "sound bites" that throw out *soul* as an incantation in commercials are backed up by ethereal choir music or hymnlike underlying melodies.

This trivialization does, I admit, annoy me. Borrowing music that was composed for the glory of God and has been sung reverently by worshipers for generations—to sell cars? Nevertheless, no one can now doubt that an awareness of something called *soul* has made it into the mainstream of our consumer culture.

TV, too, has seen a resurgence of interest in the soul in its daily programming. *The Oprah Winfrey Show* is, of course, the best example.

I am no talk-show fan. But lately I have occasionally tuned in to Oprah Winfrey's "Change Your Life" TV series. And I have to agree with a statement she made on a recent interview: TV has become the most powerful medium for our particular time—in its ability to change lives on an enormous scale.

Winfrey not only has seen the light in her own life—she's determined to enable as many as possible to benefit from the spiritual insights that have freed her from past abuse, self-loathing, and despair. Her intelligent, sincere enthusiasm conveys beautifully how, for her, "a desire realized is sweet to the soul." She has not only survived, but is in a truly key position to help millions of other people do so.

She spoke on her show one afternoon of coming across an old suicide note she had written (not that many years ago) when she was at her heaviest and most desperate. Her beautiful face glowed with confession as she dispensed hope to the many people who daily watch her show—some while they hang precariously from the ends of their own personal ropes, poised to let go. There is no doubt that *she saves lives*—with God's help.

It is an awesome sight to see an entire Chicago studio audience holding outstretched palms and praying together, in one voice, asking God to *come into their hearts,* to change them, to renew them, to use them in the world!

I have been blessed seeing Oprah reading from her favorite Psalms as a meditation at the end of the hour show. She generously passes on compassionate advice to help needy, seeking souls come face-to-face with the God who has been seeking them all of their lives.

All I can say is, "Preach it, Sister!" And may all sincere seekers take the steps that will lead them beyond the much-needed milk of sustenance . . . to the meat of the Gospel . . . and an even deeper understanding of discipleship as they grow in grace.

It's like church on a weekday afternoon! And are viewers complaining, asking for more fashion advice and ways to get back at their mothers-in-law? (For such, turn to Sally or Jenny.) NO! Oprah remains on top of the ratings heap. The prophets would have been envious.

Oprah would be among the first to admit that, from the point at which she began her life, the way up has been a steady climb. Yet it is also true that the one criterion for God's using us is *our willingness to accept help.* According to the Apostle Paul, we shouldn't be surprised that God chooses to "partner" with the likes of us. God is always in the business of raising up the weak and the unlikely to amaze the "wise" (the philosophically and theologically trained?) and the "noble" (even royalty has had to give Oprah her due).

The real power that enables life to go on, that strengthens individual souls to rise above the chasm of shame and blame, that confounds nations and brings light to the people—is *the power of God within us.* It is not rational arguments or measured solutions or scientific data. Of course, God is pleased to use *all* of these *as they are useful* for the redemption of human life day to day.

But . . .

a small child who gives her life to God at the end of a Sunday School prayer . . .

the housewife who seeks to practice one act of kindness every day (as she is encouraged to do by Oprah's "Angel Network") . . .

the businessman who decides not to use his power unfairly against a rival—*these are the blessed.*

These are the new bearers of wisdom. These are the ones who will inherit the Kingdom. By partnering with God in seeking to stand up against the darkness, they spread the light. And that light is always Christ.

I still have problems with "sound bites." Little tantalizing clips of news and programming notes that you must STAY TUNED to discover the full explanation of. Oprah, like the rest of the media, has been criticized for catering to the hip and the popularizers to get her message across. Since I am not responsible for attaining the ratings that keep one on the air, I cannot imagine the pressure it must entail to use sound bites responsibly without "selling your soul." I only know what I see when

I turn on the tube, and as often as not I turn it off again immediately.

But soul sound bites seem to be here to stay. Books with the word "soul" in them garner immediate attention. So perhaps even the most trivial suggestion that something conveys "soul" or heals the soul can be a stepping-stone on a path to seeking stronger sustenance. Those who know they have a greater emptiness than the everyday fare can satisfy can go as deep as they wish, investigating many sources—the Bible, in any edition imaginable, being foremost on the list.

I am glad that (in the words of Patrick Glynn), "at the end of the twentieth century, modern psychology has found what we might call telltale signs of the soul"—a universal "hunger" or drive that sends humans to seek a relationship with the Divine. Now perhaps many are ready for revitalization of the classical spiritual terms—such as faith, grace, hope—as their souls long for *"more."*

Signs of Soul

Medicine . . . is on the verge of a postsecular revolution. It is rediscovering the soul. As Harvard Medical School associate professor of medicine Herbert Benson puts it, contemporary medical research is showing that the human mind and body are "wired for God."

—Patrick Glynn

I will write it on their hearts; and I will be their God, and
they shall be my people. . . . For they shall all know me,
from the least of them to the greatest, says the Lord.
—Jeremiah 31:33,34

Chapter Eighteen

My earliest recollection, perhaps, was a fuzzy but pivotal realization that *God was great and I was not.* I don't believe I was even in Sunday School yet. I know it was well before school-age (I never went to kindergarten, but began first grade in parochial school when I was five). I remember playing on a hardwood floor somewhere in one of our first homes, winding up a small painted-tin, church-shaped music box. It was clearly a symbol of the holy—it played "Jesus Loves Me."

Somehow in the throes of play, in my child's world, I began—gathering together whatever I conceived to be "myself"—a soul's journey that continues today. The "I—Thou" relationship that was struck up like a fire being suddenly kindled (or slowly brought to a point of boiling?) was as much—more—a reality to me than any physical fact of my childhood I can recall.

In fact, other than another early recollection of rolling Easter eggs around the same floor—I remember few overwhelmingly concrete details of growing up as a quiet, shy only child. But the memory of knowing that GOD WAS . . . is still as crisp and convincing as a photograph that has gradually developed before my eyes.

Because this is my naive and unretouched experience, I did not find it surprising but only corroborating to read that: "The knowledge of Spirit is prior to the knowledge of reason. Where reason follows Spirit, the results are good; where it rejects or parts ways with Spirit, the results are inevitably disastrous, whether one speaks of the political, societal, or personal spheres. Reason rediscovers and reconstructs in slow, cumbersome, linear, and partial fashion what Spirit already knows."[1]

I could not have explained it that way myself, even now. But reading the statement affirms what St. John of the Cross says (in *Ascent of Mount Carmel):* "In every soul, even that of the greatest sinner in the world, God dwells, and is substantially present. This way of union or presence of God, in the order of nature, subsists between Him and all His creatures." To have realized it so young is "mere grace"; to have the privilege of living decade after decade in awareness of *being* a soul with God *is life itself.*

"But, as it is written, 'What no eye has seen, nor ear heard, nor the human heart conceived, what God has prepared for those who love him'—these things God has revealed to us through the Spirit; for the Spirit searches everything, even the depths of God. . . . And we speak of these things in words not taught by human wisdom but taught by the Spirit, interpreting spiritual things to those who are spiritual."[2]

And: "For what can be known about God is plain to them, because God has shown it to them. Ever since the creation of the world his eternal power and divine nature, invisible though they are, have been understood and seen through the things he has made."[3]

This I have always believed—not because I started out with the verses and the "proof." Rather, this explanation is the only thread running through all of reality that makes sense of any of it—that as human beings we have been, from the beginning, *designed by and "wired for God."*

Patrick Glynn offers several themes, not "proofs" of God's existence, but areas of support for what he insists is the soul's intimate and certain knowledge of this I—Thou relationship:

The first is cosmological. Although twentieth-century intellectuals have commonly spoken of the "random universe," Brandon Carter, an astrophysicist and cosmologist from Cambridge University has written of "The Anthropic Principle in Cosmology." His insights, presented 500 years after Copernicus, according to Glynn, "spelled nothing less than the philosophical overthrow of the Copernican revolution itself."

"Anthropic principle," from the Greek word *anthropos*, "man," consists of the observation that "what we can expect to observe [in the universe] must be restricted by the conditions necessary for our presence as observers." In other, plainer words, it affirms that all the seemingly arbitrary and ostensibly unrelated constants in physics have one strange factor in common: They happen to be precisely the values you need *if you want to have a universe capable of producing life.*

In essence, this comes down to the growing realization that the many laws of physics were somehow "fine-tuned" from the beginning of the universe to result in life as we know it. In fact, it is embarrassingly evident to some who do not wish to frame it this way that: the universe we inhabit *appears to be precisely planned to accommodate the emergence of human beings.*

People had interpreted Copernicus's theory to mean that humans had no "privileged *central* place in the universe," as Carter put it. But the explanation was not so simple. Too many values in physics had been arranged around the central task of *producing us.* So even if our position in the universe is not *central* (we must humbly admit)—it's as though Someone had Something in mind, *and we are it.*

The signs are everywhere, from something as seemingly inconsequential as my little music box that played *Jesus loves me, this I know . . .* to the cosmos itself. Sometimes life does bring us full circle. That blessed naiveté on the other side of experience, philosophy, reason—is the most precious of all. Actually, I have a much harder time believing in somehow spontaneous, godless origins of life—than I have resting in the assurance that "God created . . . " While the ancient affirmation "God created . . . " *is* poetry, it is also Beauty and Truth. And so, knowing that *God is*, and that therefore *I am*—it is well with my soul.

[1]*God: The Evidence,* p. 166.

[2]1 Corinthians 2:9–10, 13.

[3]Romans 1:20.

Jesus and the Soul

No one after lighting a lamp puts it under the bushel basket, but on the lampstand, and it gives light to all in the house. In the same way, let your light shine before others . . . and give glory to your Father in heaven.

—Jesus, Matthew 5:15-16

Thou thyself, must go through Christ's whole journey,
and enter wholly into his process.
—Jacob Boehme,
True Repentance

Chapter Nineteen

*A*nother "sign of the soul" that has come to light in recent years is the reporting of "near-death" and actual death experiences—which have included out-of-body floating sensations and even the viewing of oneself on an operating table during surgery.

I confess I have *not* had an out-of-body or near-death experience, had waking visions, caught glimpses of angels—or heard celestial voices at any time. Rather, the depths of many of my dream-wanderings, what I have read and seen and heard, and my experiences of soul moments through the years alone convince me.

But what of those who *have* seen and heard? Patrick Glynn in *God: The Evidence* writes extensively of the "second sign" of soul [the first being modern physics]. What of the "intimations of immortality" that are inherent in the near-death experience? People who have "come back," as reported by authors such as

Raymond Moody, have sometimes described the dying process. They spoke not only of "floating" out of their bodies (they=their souls), but of observing medical procedures being performed on them—from a viewpoint they could not possibly have had while on the table, unconscious—and with details about medical technique they could not have understood.

Some reported whooshing rapidly down a dark corridor or tunnel toward a point of light. At the end of the tunnel they would encounter a heavenly landscape and a "Being of Light" whom many identified as Christ himself. Colors around them glowed in supernaturally vivid brilliance. The intensity of the light was immense, yet it did not hurt their eyes.

Just last night, while I was channel-surfing, I happened upon a movie about one such death-survivor who (according to the story) had been struck by lightning, had died and then come back with intense ESP and the ability to help other people during the dying process. There was even an actor playing the author Raymond Moody who corroborated the man's experiences.

Danny, the returned-from-death character, said that once people had experienced this wonderful out-of-body peace and fulfillment, they did not fear death again after coming back to life. In the movie, he dies a second time, on an operating table. He is able to hear an attending doctor say, "I bet twenty bucks he won't make it!" Later, having come back yet again, he is eating a meal in the cafeteria with this doctor. Danny hands him a twenty-dollar bill and says, "Here, Doc, you won. I *did* die on the table but I got sent back." The doctor is mortified and apologizes profusely.

All of these details are consistent with actual reports of extra-sensory awareness—such as patients knowing who is in the waiting room while they are in surgery, being aware of things going on throughout the hospital.

One interesting thing is that while some of the details of death experiences *do* fit the images and teachings of the Bible (the importance of light, of love), there is enough after-life affirmation experienced by everyone—believers and unbelievers alike—to have made some church leaders skeptical and even angry. Do Near Death Experiences (NDEs) take the wind out of the church's sails? What if *everyone* finds eventual peace without some kind of repentance and forgiveness having taken place while in the body?

But some fewer patients have reported having hellish experiences. They have experienced desperation for a chance to repent and change their ways (again, like the rich man who ignored Lazarus)—which most have done religiously upon returning to "life." Some people also report having had "life reviews" in which all of their lives flashed before them, meetings with those who were closely linked to their lives, and an awareness of how they affected those people by their actions, good and bad.

But what about the Jesus-figure that so many find welcoming their souls to the other side? The concept of a reckoning for the good and evil done in one's life has always been part of the NDEs. Lives seem to be reviewed by Christ or "The Light," but not with a judgmental spirit. Rather, people who have died and come back experience at once a firm, uncompromising sense of right and wrong, grounded in a Law of Love which the New Testament Christ propounded. While there is embarrassment and shame during their all-revealing "life review," there is also a sense of acceptance, over-whelming forgiveness, unity with other souls, and in many cases a renewed determination to thereafter *structure their whole lives around Love* as the only true value in the universe.

Betty J. Eadie reports in *Embraced by the Light:*

"As I remained in the Savior's glow, in his absolute love, I realized that when I had feared him as a child I had actually moved myself further from him. When I thought he didn't love me, I was moving my love from him. He never moved. I saw now that he was like a sun in my galaxy. I moved all around him, sometimes nearer and sometimes farther away, but his love never failed."[1]

Glynn reports one story told by George Ritchie about his 1943 near-death encounter with a "Man made out of light." When Ritchie is given the message that life is really about loving other human beings, he thinks, "Someone should have told me!" What he hears in response from the Being is: *I did tell you . . . I told you by the life I lived. I told you by the death I died.*

What did Jesus really teach about the soul? To me the essence of it is found in Matthew 5 in the Sermon on the Mount. When he proclaimed that the "poor in spirit" are the blessed ones, the ones who have found the way to true life, it flew right in the face of the classical worldview that pride in oneself was the "crown of the virtues." Glynn writes, "In the classical under-standing, the strong, the beautiful, the intelligent, the rich were not just better off but *morally* better than the weak, the poor, the meek, the downtrodden." You even find some of this thinking in the Psalms in which the life of prosperity is equated with God's blessing (cf. Ps.128).

Why are gifts not given to us all equally? Why does God allow suffering? These are the eternal questions, as old as the Book of Job. And, as much as we would wish to have sweeping, conclusive answers: we are most likely to reach *any* understanding only *in the moment,* as Job did when confronted with God's great and inexplicable work in the universe (ch. 38f).

As modern seekers too have discovered, *experience speaks volumes.* Betty Eadie continues to relate her conclusions from her death experience (none of which she had studied or read or even thought about in her earlier life):

"Now I knew that there actually was a God. No longer did I believe in just a Universal Power, but now I saw the Man behind that Power. I saw a loving Being who created the universe and placed all knowledge within it. I saw that he governs this knowledge and controls its power. I understood with pure knowledge that God wants us to become as he is, and that he has invested us with god-like qualities, such as the power of imagination and creation, free will, intelligence, and most of all, the power to love. I understood that he actually *wants* us to draw on the powers of heaven, and that by *believing* that we are capable of doing so, we can."[2]

This awareness need not come to us in a death or near-death experience. As the rich man was told, those on earth have the Law and the Prophets. The Word is out there, as are other experienced souls. It is possible to stumble onto the Way . . . to find peace of soul and grow to be *limned by love.* All we have to do is be "poor in spirit" and ask, and the powers of heaven are available to help us take the next step . . . and the next.

Each of us is *a soul on a journey* in which we will, to some degree, recapitulate the actions and experiences of Christ himself, when he was on earth. As Emily Dickinson wrote: "Gethsemane and Cana/Are still a traveled route." He too was dependent on his Heavenly

Father when he was in the flesh, dwelling among us. He too was tempted by the things of the world (though without sin). He was belittled, abused, betrayed. . . . He knew loneliness, hunger, and the dark. Yet he prayed, "Father, forgive them."

Christ is ever the soul's friend, for whatever comes . . . on whichever side of the veil. Yet to choose intentionally, faithfully, to identify with him *in this life*—as a "man [or woman] for others"—is to become, to some degree, even here and now, *with him, a being of light.*

[1]*Embraced by the Light* (Bantam, 1994), p. 60.
[2]p. 61.

A Far Country

The access to heaven is through desire. He who longs to be there really is there in spirit. The path of Heaven is measured by desire and not by miles.

—The Cloud of
Unknowing

Man must eat in order to live . . . and the whole world is presented as one all-embracing banquet table. . . . This image of the banquet remains, throughout the whole Bible, the central image of life. It is the image of life at its creation and also the image of life at its end and fulfillment: ". . . that you eat and drink at my table in my Kingdom."
—Alexander Schmemann

Chapter Twenty

$\mathcal{I}$n a (as yet unpublished) novel, *Encounters on the Far Shore,* I wrote a story of various figures coming into a "far country" where life was (as in the near-death experience) too vivid for accurate description. Only metaphor suffices. There the characters I envisioned are tested in their "desire" for the true fulfillment of all souls: union with God in ever-increasing beauty, knowledge, and joy. Some of them keep using the same old rationalizations that served to keep them separated from other people on earth; a few begin to see and accept the Light, and choose to journey on into the Country that is measured by desire and not by miles . . .

In Luke 14, Jesus, continuing to speak in parables, told of a man who gave a wedding banquet and sent his underlings to call all who had been invited to the event. But they began to make excuses as to why they could not come. The would-be host became enraged, and told his servant, "Go out at once into the streets and lanes of the town and bring in the poor, the crippled, the blind and the lame."

In a similar but more shocking version of the story, Matthew's Gospel tells of a king who invited guests who not only refused to come, but became abusive to those serving under them, and then received retribution from the king. But, as in the other story, *there still were no guests.* So this king also told his servants to go to the main streets and invite everyone they found to the wedding banquet. Soon the prepared hall was filled with people.

But when the king himself arrived, he noticed that there was a man without a proper wedding robe. So he asked, "Friend, how did you get in here without a robe?" And, cruelly it seems, the king had his attendants bind the man hand and foot, and throw him out into—not just street darkness—but "outer darkness."

This second banquet parable—especially if the king in any way represents God—is a real affront to our sensibilities. What could the garment be, and why does the soul need it? More to the point, how could one be expected to have such a crucial item without being tipped off beforehand . . . and without being the kind of person who could *acquire* such a garment in the first place? (These folk were the "good and bad," gathered from the streets.)

Jesus' parables were often designed to offend, to wake up complacent religious people who figured they were "shoo-ins" for God's Kingdom by virtue of their birthright. No sweat. Plus, they lived the good life, following the commandments, and especially teaching others to toe the line (though surely *they* were entitled to *some* privileges, being as high up as they were!).

So who "makes it" to the far country? If the soul is created with intimate relationality to God, and, through the course of an earthly journey, this spiritual link seems to be forgotten, or to grow weak, or to become obscured in forgetfulness and doubt and disillusionment—what next? How can *such souls as we all are* be expected to show up for the Banquet at the End of Time?

Popular author Robert Farrar Capon takes a new and ingenuous tack in answering such a question—one that resonates with my soul. He writes in *The Romance of the Word* that for a long time he has felt that the problems of modern theology could be solved more easily with "a reworking of the notion of *sacramentality*" than by contrived theological explanations. Capon pulls It All together, in his own words, by "the bright idea of saving all of orthodox theology and solving all the problems of the modern critics in one fell swoop: *If God in Christ didn't do the job of saving the world in a way we can see, he did it in a way we can't see—in the Mystery of Christ.*" And his "device" for effecting this solution is "the standard catholic notion of *sacrament,* slightly reworked and extended."

He begins with his own shocking statement that a sacrament is never a transaction. When we receive Christ's body and blood in the Eucharist, it is not as though we didn't have it before. We do not receive an *accretion* of Jesus, he insists—like a refill at the service station. Despite the lostness we might feel, Jesus never left our soul. In fact, playfully painting his own version of the banquet, he says we must affirm regarding the sacrament that: *"It's a party the church is already at and not some limousine that brings Jesus to the church's door."*

Likewise, in the other sacraments, "The church doesn't take Jesus to the heathen: Jesus, because he is God, is already intimately and immediately present to the heathen before we arrive." Jesus is God-with-us as Friend of the soul, as Creator and Redeemer in all his power. Jesus is the Light of the world, says Capon, "not the Lighting Company of the world." Neither he nor his Church is an electricity source that you have to get hooked up to in order to have light in your life. "He is the Sun, not a power utility; all you have to do is trust in him enough to open your eyes and presto! You had light all along."[*]

Likewise, for Capon, salvation through Christ is no remedy offered by God late in the game, but rather the "Grand Mystery" underlying all our history. A possible answer to *What is that mysterious wedding garment that every soul must have?* is starting to emerge. It's beginning to sound more and more as though the *desire* spoken of in that mystical classic, *The Cloud of Unknowing,* as an access to heaven (see quote at the beginning of this chapter)—is more than metaphorical. When we acknowledge such desire as *what one must bring to the Banquet,* reality becomes much more hopeful for us all.

What is this Desire that secures us, the "poor in spirit," a seat at the table . . . that allows us to walk on, all the way into the Kingdom (which Jesus also said is within us and all around us right now)? *It is a way of life for the soul*—not just gaining knowledge, not just trying to act rightly, to keep aware, to love others as ourselves, to grow in the Spirit—though it is all of these things. It is the purest intimacy that flows between lovers: the experience of knowing Jesus as the Lover of our soul, the one who "rocks" us and holds us like a weaned child—who nurtures and values us in the particularity and completeness each of us possesses through grace.

As C. S. Lewis has the great teacher George Macdonald say in his afterlife novel, *The Great Divorce:* "Hell is a state of mind . . . and every state of mind, left to itself, every shutting up of the creature within the dungeon of its own mind—is, in the end Hell. But Heaven is not a state of mind. Heaven is reality itself. All that is fully real is heavenly."*

Soul moments are real moments that we may experience every day—affirmations of the true touching of heaven to earth. *You know them when they occur. Why not name them?* Let us all listen to our hearts, fall in love and *stay* in love with God, and learn to foster the connections between our natural lives and the world of the Spirit throughout all the years we are allotted. As A. W. Tozer put it, "Life in the presence of God should be enjoyed every moment of every day."

The Great Divorce (Macmillan, 1946).

Sharing Your Soul Moments

If you would like to tell us of times in your life when "heaven touched earth" . . . and you caught a glimpse of something God was showing you beyond the ordinary . . . perhaps an event or insight that brought new joy, understanding, and spiritual connection to your life:

Send your stories of Soul Moments, in 250 words or less, to Isabel Anders at **soulstories@andersgroup.com**. Some contributions may be selected for inclusion in a new book of Soul Moments.

Visit Isabel Anders' website at **www.andersgroup.com**.